CAROLINE WREY'S

Finishing Touches

CAROLINE WREY'S
Finishing Touches

INSPIRATIONAL IDEAS AND 25 STEP-BY-STEP PROJECTS

TO ENHANCE YOUR HOME

Joanne
yours
Caroline Wrey

COLLINS & BROWN

I dedicate this book to my three children, Harry, Rachel and Humphrey.
I hope that they will enjoy creating their homes as much as I have.

First published in Great Britain in 1999
by Collins & Brown Limited
London House
Great Eastern Wharf
Parkgate Road
London SW11 4NQ

1 3 5 7 9 8 6 4 2

British Library Cataloguing-in-Publication Data:
A catalogue record for this book
is available from the British Library.

ISBN 1 85585 722 7 (hardback edition)
ISBN 1 85585 749 9 (paperback edition)

Conceived, edited and designed by Collins & Brown Limited

Editor: Kate Haxell
Designer: Janet James
Photography: Lucinda Symons
Stylist: Lucinda Egerton
Step-by-step photography: Sampson Lloyd

Reproduction by Hong Kong Graphic & Printing Ltd
Printed and bound in China by Sun Fung Ltd

Distributed in the United States and Canada by Sterling Publishing Co,
387 Park Avenue South, New York, NY 10016, USA

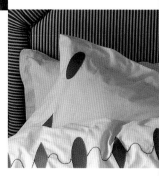

Contents

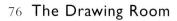

Introduction

In any room you always have decorating boundaries of some description, usually either architecture, budget or inherited curtains, carpets or pieces of furniture. However, these boundaries are often useful starting points on which you can then build. The prorities and boundaries in a room should not be obvious to an outsider, since the overall look should be highly successful and very easy to live with.

Fabric and trimming choices, together with the natural play of light upon them, hold a pretty significant place in a room. The window treatment is probably of primary importance, but it is everything else, all those delicious individual touches, which then create a gentle harmony and easy equilibrium within the room. The curtains, and their pelmet, should be reflected in the other items in the room in terms of style, colour, texture and eye-catching detail. The furniture, pictures, pretty ornaments, lampshades, cushions, tassels and flowers must all combine to create that wonderfully special ambience that makes a room such a pleasure to spend time in. It is lovely to walk into a room and feast your eyes on a wide variety of items that all tie in with each other.

There is no doubt that a perfect room makes you feel deeply happy, which, spiritually, is an extremely good thing. Therefore, it is worth focusing your attention on the production of the goodies in this book. From a wonderful buttoned cushion to a stunning gothic screen, most of the projects are so easy to execute – each item merely requiring a little organization to put it together successfully. Some of the projects are more challenging, such as the smart pleated headboard and the elegant silk lampshade. However, none of them require any special skills, just attention to detail and a methodical approach. Follow the clear step-by-step instructions carefully and each item will not only be fun to make, it will also look completely brilliant and very professional. And remember, you, as the creator, can influence any room through your finishing touches.

Caroline Wrey

THE Living ROOM

The way the light falls in a room is so important in creating the right ambience and, therefore, the window treatment is of paramount importance in terms of controlling the light. This room has a low, beamed ceiling, but as it is a living room, used a lot during the day, it is essential that it gets the maximum available light. To this end, the pelmet board is set as high as possible and the pelmet itself is shallow, so we lose the minimum amount of light. The natural-coloured rope and fringe details look particularly good here since the house is in the country. It is amazing how easy it is to make cottage proportions look large and elegant just by the use, or introduction, of elements in the room.

Thick interlined curtains give a sumptuous air to this room. The band, cut on the diagonal, adds a wonderfully interesting detail to the window treatment as a whole, as does the jute rope, used here instead of piping. In addition, the jute fringe gives a lovely soft look to the lower edge of the pelmet skirt, and the plaited jute tiebacks are a perfect addition to the overall design.

All these natural materials blend beautifully with the colour and texture of the fabric. The look is informal but elegant and coolly sophisticated; perfectly offsetting the rest of the goodies in the room, such as the luxurious envelope cushion and the slender furniture. All very inviting.

The Classic Curtain

Nothing beats the look of a curtain that has been beautifully made with good interlining. This is a simple project to make – do not be put off by its size. Two pairs of clamps, a long ruler and a large table will help you to make any curtain, however big, with ease.

MATERIALS

Main fabric   *8cm (3in) pencil-pleat tape*
Lining   *Lead weights*
Medium interlining   *Brass hooks*

MEASURING

Length: *measure from the floor to the top of the window (see page 123).*

Width: *the length of the rail or pole plus housing space on each side (see page 123).*

CUTTING THE FABRICS

For each curtain

Main fabric length: *to the finished drop add 20cm (8in): 12cm (5in) for the hem and 8cm (3in) for the turn-down at the top. I add a further 1cm (½in) as I like the curtains to just 'break' on the floor.*

Main fabric width: *two-and-a-half times the length of the pelmet board divided by two. Pattern match (see page 40) and machine stitch the drops together. When pulling up the pencil-pleat tape allow an extra 10cm (4in) on top of the measured finished width of each curtain. This will allow the curtain to cover the added distance across the overlap arm of the rail and the returns to the wall.*

Interlining length: *10cm (4in) shorter than the main fabric.*

Interlining width: *the same as the main fabric.*

Lining length: *10cm (4in) shorter than the main fabric.*

Lining width: *the same as the main fabric.*

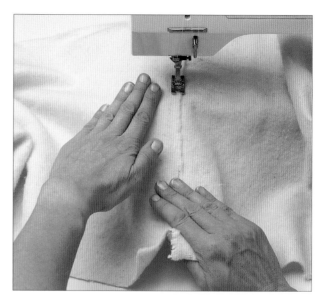

1 Join the drops of interlining for one curtain by overlapping the fabric by 1.5cm (⅝in) and stitching them together with the biggest zigzag setting on your machine. You do not need to pin beyond the first 30cm (12in). Do not worry if this seam does not come out completely straight and even, as it will be incorporated invisibly into the curtain.

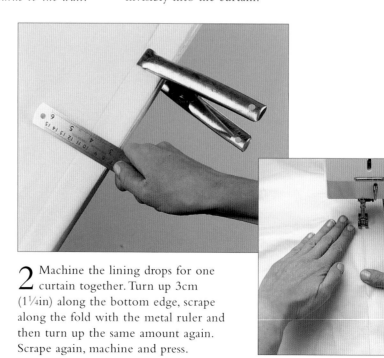

2 Machine the lining drops for one curtain together. Turn up 3cm (1¼in) along the bottom edge, scrape along the fold with the metal ruler and then turn up the same amount again. Scrape again, machine and press.

3 Clamp the side edge of the interlining to the edge of the table and lay the main fabric for one curtain on top of it, right side up. Place the top of the main fabric 8cm (3in) above the top of the interlining. Fold back the side edge of the main fabric until you reach the middle of the interlining. Make interlocking stitches (see page 125) 10cm (4in) apart down the folded edge, joining the main fabric to the interlining. Start and stop 20cm (8in) from the top and bottom of the interlining. Repeat this row of interlocking vertically down the curtain, parallel to the selvedge, approximately every 40cm (16in), from the fold to 40cm (16in) from one edge. Move to the other side of the table and repeat the process to interlock the whole curtain. Turn the curtain over so the main fabric is now right side down.

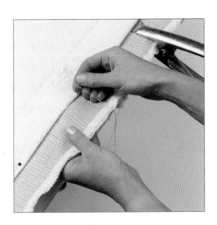

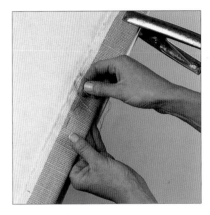

4 Fold back the interlining 5cm (2in) at the leading edge of the curtain, ready for more interlocking stitches. The easiest way to do this is to slip the little metal ruler between the interlining and the main fabric and fold back and pin the interlining at the 5cm (2in) mark.

5 Make another row of interlocking stitches along this fold, starting and stopping 20cm (8in) from the top and bottom of the curtain. Make these stitches approximately 5cm (2in) apart as the leading edge must be very secure.

6 Turn the main fabric over the interlining down the leading edge and anchor it with pyramid stitches (see page 125). Start and stop 20cm (8in) from the top and bottom. Clamp the fabric edge to the table in sections and work, with one hand under the fabric, between the clamps. Repeat steps 4, 5 and 6 on the other side of the curtain.

7 Turn up 12cm (4¾in) along the bottom edge of the curtain. Measure with the little metal ruler and pin horizontally close to the fold (see detail). At the corner just turn up 12cm (4¾in) of fabric at this stage.

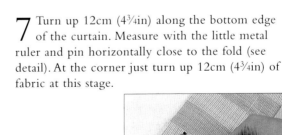

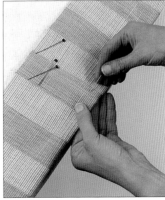

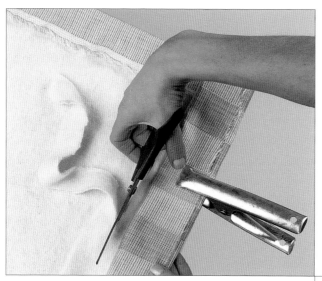

8 Fold back the edge of the main fabric and trim away 3cm (1¼in) of the interlining.

9 Turn under 3cm (1¼in) of the main fabric, folding it over the raw edge of the interlining inside the hem. Pin the folded edge, moving the pins up from the bottom edge. The hem will measure approximately 9cm (3½in). Leave 30cm (12in) in from each corner un-pinned.

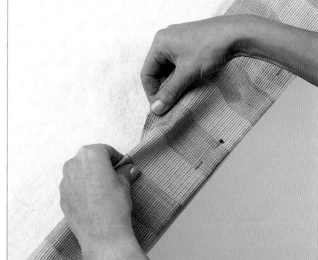

10 Lay the corner on top of the corner of your worksurface to check that it is a right angle. Smooth out any rucks within the fold with closed scissor blades and then mark the corner with a pin stuck deeply in.

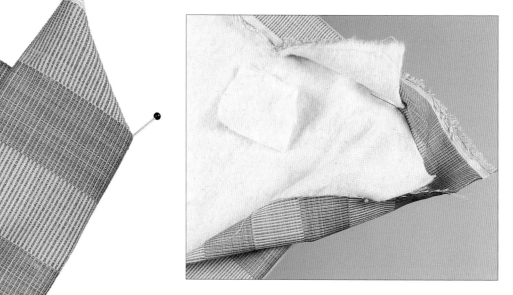

11 Open the hem and side seam out flat and cut off a rectangle of the interlining as shown. Cut around the outside edge of the pin marking the corner.

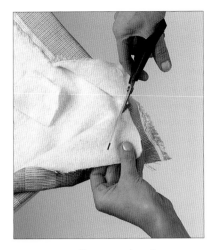

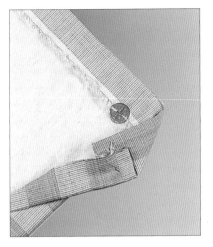

12 Cut off a triangle of interlining from the pin marking the corner to the bottom edge of the interlining, at approximately a 45° angle. It is vital to remove this bulk properly to achieve a professional-looking, neat corner.

13 From the leading edge, fold the main fabric over in a neat triangle at 90° to the edge of the curtain. With doubled button thread, stitch a lead weight in the fold of the hem. Make four stitches in each hole, going over the edge of the weight as shown. Fold the hem and side seam back into place.

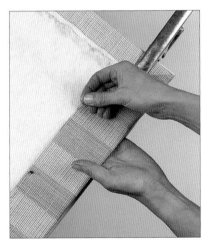

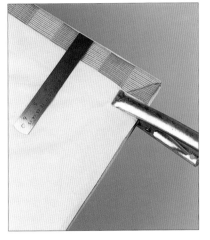

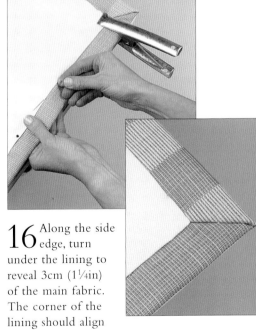

14 Slip stitch (see page 125) the hem, working up the diagonal from the corner and along the top edge. Move the clamps along as you work to keep the fabric flat and in position; this is an enormous help to the speed and success of your sewing. Use a long slim needle at all times but especially when slip stitching, as the length of the needle allows you to make longer stitches. You will soon achieve an easy, quick rhythm and acquire a natural tension to your hand stitches.

15 Align one of the raw edges of the lining with the side of the curtain. At the bottom, leave 3cm (1¼in) of the main fabric hem showing below the hemmed lining. Clamp the lining in position.

16 Along the side edge, turn under the lining to reveal 3cm (1¼in) of the main fabric. The corner of the lining should align with the corner fold in the main fabric. Slip stitch 3cm (1¼in) of the lining to the main fabric along the hem to the corner, then stitch up the side edge. Keep a hand under the curtain to ensure that no stitches come through to the front. Stop stitching 20cm (8in) from the top.

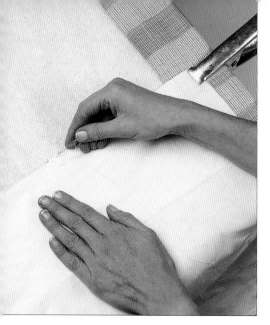

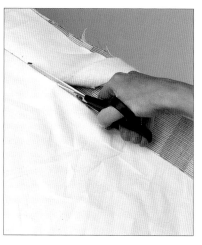

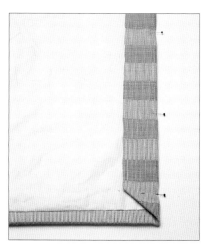

17 Interlock the lining to the interlining every 40cm (16in), but do not worry about positioning the rows of stitches over the previous interlocking stitches. At the bottom edge make a few good anchor stitches, as this is the only place where the lining is joined to the hem. When all the rows of interlocking stitches are completed, trim off excess lining on the other side of the curtain, so that the raw edge is aligned with the edge of the curtain, and repeat steps 15 and 16 on the other side edge of the curtain.

18 Measure from the hem up the curtain to the finished drop measurement. Draw a line in pen across the curtain at this point and cut away the excess lining and interlining. Be careful not to cut the main fabric.

19 Turn down the main fabric and fold in the corners at 45°. Pin in place, with the pins running vertically down from the top.

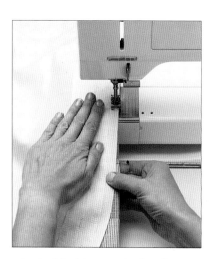

20 Machine on the heading tape, with the top edge aligned with the top of the curtain. Turn under 1cm (½in) at each end of the tape before you start and pull the three cords free at one end, ready for pulling up the curtain.

21 Pull up the cords until the curtain is the desired width (remembering to add 10cm (4in) as described in *Cutting The Fabrics*). You can clamp one edge of the curtain to the worksurface and pull up the cords from the other side if you find this easier.

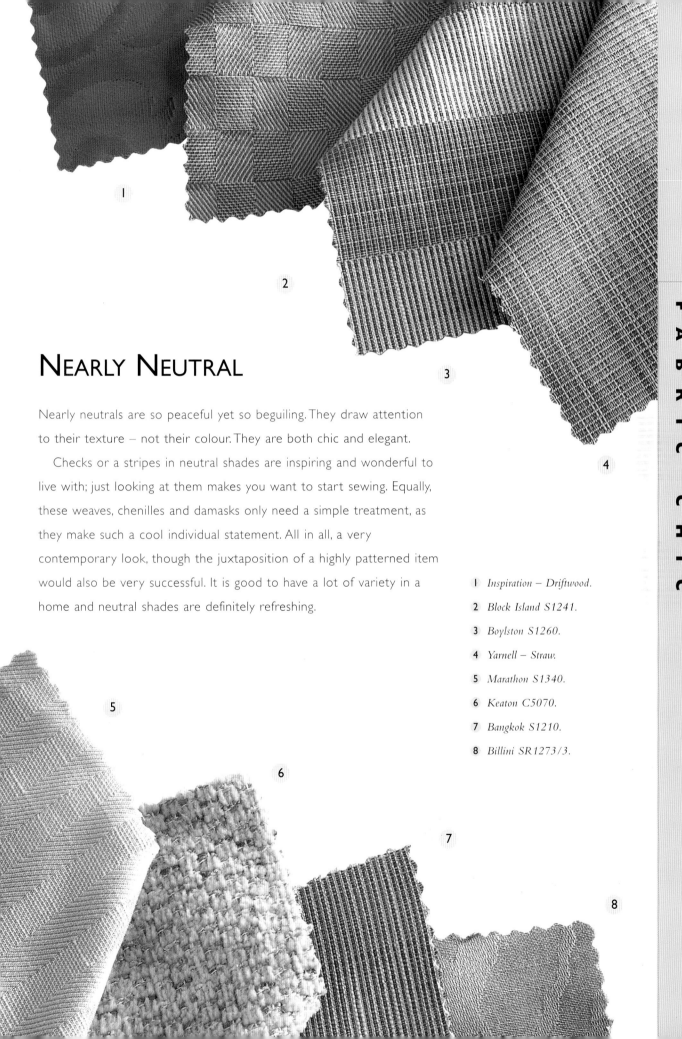

NEARLY NEUTRAL

Nearly neutrals are so peaceful yet so beguiling. They draw attention to their texture — not their colour. They are both chic and elegant.

Checks or a stripes in neutral shades are inspiring and wonderful to live with; just looking at them makes you want to start sewing. Equally, these weaves, chenilles and damasks only need a simple treatment, as they make such a cool individual statement. All in all, a very contemporary look, though the juxtaposition of a highly patterned item would also be very successful. It is good to have a lot of variety in a home and neutral shades are definitely refreshing.

1 *Inspiration – Driftwood.*

2 *Block Island S1241.*

3 *Boylston S1260.*

4 *Yarnell – Straw.*

5 *Marathon S1340.*

6 *Keaton C5070.*

7 *Bangkok S1210.*

8 *Billini SR1273/3.*

Banded Pelmet with Soft Skirt

This is such a perfect pelmet design for a low-ceilinged room. The skirt must be double, or more, the depth of the band, but this is the only restriction, making it an extremely versatile design in terms of proportions and added details. The fusible buckram is an essential ingredient in the band and gives it the necessary stability for the ultimate professional look.

MATERIALS

Main fabric

Lining

2cm (³⁄4in) wide sew-on Velcro

Jute fringe

Interlining

Fusible buckram

Jute rope

MEASURING

Length: *one-sixth of the drop of the total window treatment.*

Width: *the length of the pelmet board plus the returns.*

CUTTING THE FABRICS

For the band

Main fabric length: *one-third of the length of the pelmet, cut on the cross (see page 41), plus 3cm (1¹⁄4in) seam allowances.*

Main fabric width: *the front of the pelmet board plus returns, plus 3cm (1¹⁄4in) seam allowances.*

Velcro: *the front of the pelmet board plus returns.*

Interlining and fusible buckram length: *3.5cm (1³⁄8in) shorter than the main fabric.*

Interlining and fusible buckram width: *3.5cm (1³⁄8in) narrower than the main fabric.*

Jute rope: *the length and width of the main fabric twice plus 10cm (4in).*

For the skirt

Main fabric length: *at least two-thirds of the length of the pelmet plus 6cm (2¹⁄2in), plus 1.5cm (⁵⁄8in) seam allowance.*

Main fabric width: *two to two-and-a-half times the finished width of the pelmet plus 6cm (2¹⁄2in) seam allowances.*

Lining length: *two-thirds the length of the pelmet minus 12cm (4³⁄4in).*

Lining width: *3cm (1¹⁄4in) narrower than the main fabric.*

Jute fringe: *the width of the main fabric plus 10cm (4in).*

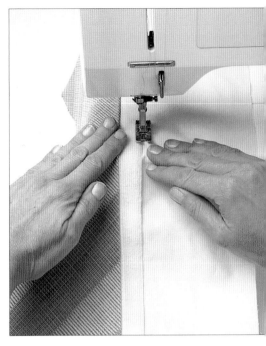

1 Right sides facing, machine the main fabric and lining of the band together along one long edge, starting and stopping 1.5cm (⅝in) from each end. Press very firmly, ensuring that the lining does not show at the front.

2 Open the band out flat, turn over and press 1.5cm (⅝in) down each side. Fold over and press the inner corners as shown.

3 Machine the Velcro to the lining exactly along the top edge. Machine along both long sides and across the short ends.

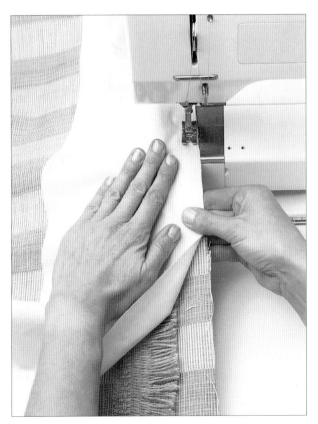

4 Either with an iron or by scraping with a small metal ruler, press a line across the main fabric of the skirt 10cm (4in) up from the bottom. Machine the jute fringe in place, with the bottom of the webbing (the braid making up the top part of the fringe) level with the pressed line.

5 Right sides facing, machine the lining to the bottom of the skirt, starting and stopping 7cm (2¾in) from each end.

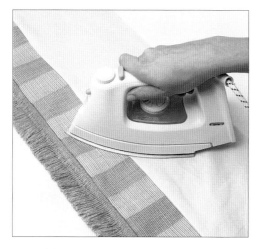

6 Fold the skirt at the pressed line and with, the fringe lying flat, press the lining seam.

7 With the skirt right side down, fold back the lining at one end and turn over and pin 1.5cm (⅝in) at the corner, as shown.

8 Turn over a double 1.5cm (⅝in) hem along the side edge of the main fabric. Fold the fringe over and tuck it neatly under the side hem. Slip stitch the side edge to the bottom hem up to the lining.

9 Turn under 1.5cm (⅝in) of the side edge of the lining and slip stitch it to the side hem of the main fabric.

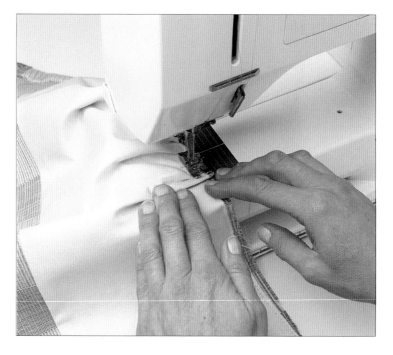

10 Along the top of the skirt, stay the stitch lining and main fabric together. Pleat up the skirt to the finished length. To help you judge this, make a mark or put a pin into the fabric every 20cm (8in). Each 20cm (8in) section must be pleated up to be 10cm (4in) long. Keep the machine running slowly and pinch up approximately 2cm (¾in) pleats and catch them in the line of machining. Keep a small bowl of water next to the machine and dampen your fingers as you pleat; this will stop the fabric slipping.

11 Open the band out flat and, right sides facing, machine the main fabric to the main fabric of the skirt.

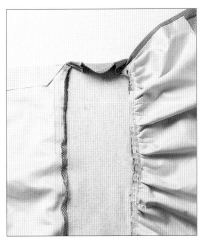

12 Lay the pelmet out right side down and place the interlining in the band, tucking it under the seam allowances.

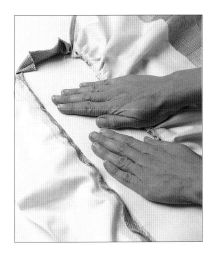

13 Place the fusible buckram over the interlining, again tucking it under the seam allowances. Make sure that there are no rucks or creases at all in the interlining or buckram.

TIP: *Traditionally this style of pelmet would be piped around the band. However, as you can see, the jute rope we have used here works perfectly. You could also use a complementary or contrasting furnishing cord in the same way.*

If you are using a trim that light will show through, such as bullion or fan edge, on the bottom of the skirt, then do not include it in the measurement of the depth of the pelmet. But if you are using a solid trim, such as a frill, then it should be included in the overall drop of the pelmet.

14 Fold the lining of the band over the buckram and iron it to fuse the buckram to the lining and interlining. Turn under, pin and slip stitch the lining of the band to the top of the skirt lining. Turn under and slip stitch the side edges of the band.

15 Stitch the jute rope around all four sides of the band. Stitch from the back of the pelmet through the underside of the rope so that the stitches don't show. Start and stop where the band joins the skirt, leaving 1cm (½in) of the rope free at each end. Tuck these raw ends to the back and catch them with a few stitches.

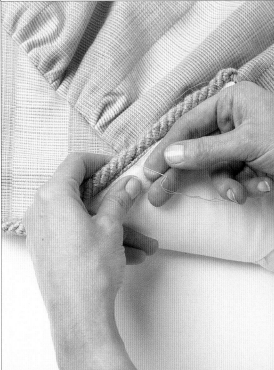

Plaited Tieback with Rosette

These are very therapeutic to make as the result is almost instantaneous and only hand sewing is involved. Once gathered and curved, the fringing converts beautifully into a rosette.

MATERIALS

Jute rope

Jute cord (alternatively, unravel a length of the rope and use a strand of that)

Jute fringe

Jute braid

Four small jute tassels

Four brass tieback rings

MEASURING

Loop a cloth tape measure around your curtain at the height you want the tieback to be. Pull the curtains back to the wall so that they hang as you wish them to. Allow enough length for the tieback to reach the hook in the wall.

CUTTING THE MATERIALS

For each tieback: three pieces of rope the measured length of the tieback plus 25%.
40cm (16in) of jute cord.
30cm (12in) of jute fringe.
12cm (4¾in) of jute braid.

1 Stitch the three lengths of rope firmly together at one end.

2 Plait the lengths together as you would plait a little girl's hair making sure the plait is tight and firm. You may find this easier if you clamp the stitched end to the side of your worksurface. When the plait is complete, stitch the ends together and trim off any excess rope.

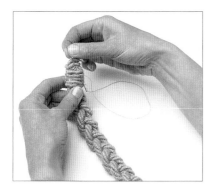

3 To bind the ends of the tieback, stitch one end of the cord to the back of the plait, 3cm (1¼in) from one end. Wind the cord around the end of the plait, stitching the loops together as you go. Tuck the loose end into the top of the binding and stitch it in place. Bind the other end of the plait in the same way.

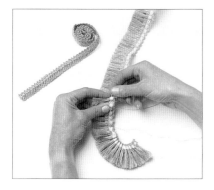

4 Gather the fringe with running stitches in the webbing. Pull it up tightly, stitch the ends at the back.

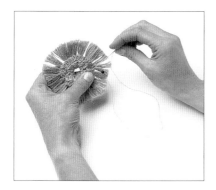

5 Turn under 0.5cm (¼in) at each end of the braid and stitch it over the inner edge of the fringe to hide the webbing. Use pins to hold it in position while you stitch. If the fringe has a decorative webbing you may not need this step.

6 Push the hanging loops of two small tassels through the hole in the centre of the rosette. Pull the tassels up and stitch the loops to the back of the rosette so that the tassels hang within the rosette at the front. Stitch the rosette to one of the bound ends. Stitch a brass ring to the back of each bound end.

Envelope Cushion

This is an easy cushion to make since there is no piping involved.
The inner cover must fit the cushion pad tightly so that the it seems to be
bursting out of the outer cover, held in place only by the pretty tassels.

MATERIALS

*Two complementary or contrasting
fabrics for the outer and inner of
the cushion*

*Two tassels on cord loops
(either purchased tassels or Arabian
tassels, see page 86)*

Cushion pad

MEASURING

The size of the cushion pad.

CUTTING THE FABRICS

Outer pieces

Length: *the length of the pad plus
10cm (4in), plus 1.5cm (⅝in)
seam allowance.*

Width: *the width of the pad plus
3cm (1¼in) seam allowances.*

Inner piece

Length: *twice the length of the pad.*

Width: *the width of the pad.*

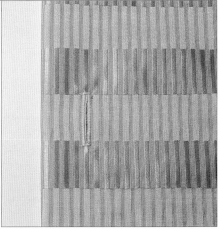

1 Zigzag along one
short edge of each
outer piece. Wrong
sides facing, turn over
the zigzagged edge
10cm (4in) and tack
it in place.

2 Fold each turned-over edge
into thirds and mark the
one-third and two-thirds folds
with pins. Make two horizontal
buttonholes at the marked
points, 2cm (¾in) in from the
turned-over edge. The buttonholes must be wide enough for
the cord loops of the tassels to
pass through easily.

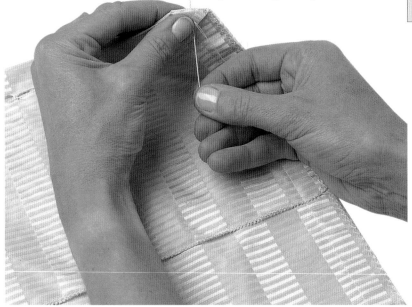

3 Place the two outer pieces
together, right sides facing and
raw edges aligning, and machine
around the three raw edges. Zigzag
close to the machine line and trim
away the excess fabric. At the open
end, fold over the seam allowance
and catch it to the line of
machining with a few tiny hand
stitches. Turn right side out.

4 Right sides facing, fold the strip of inner fabric in half and machine down the sides, taking a 1cm (½in) seam allowance. Zigzag close to the machine line and trim away the excess fabric. Turn right side out.

5 Slip the inner over the cushion pad and oversew the raw edge closed. Slip the outer over the inner the opposite way, so that the folded end of the inner protrudes from the open end of the outer. Thread the tassel cords through the buttonholes then loop them over the tassels themselves.

A **TABLE** DISPLAY

The living room is often the most formal room in the house: it is a room where you spend a huge amount of time, not just relaxing but entertaining as well. It may well be the first room that any visitor to your house will see and therefore it is important to spend time and effort getting the details right.

Obviously the soft furnishings are very important, but having got those right, turn your attention to other objects in the room. An attractive display provides a focus point, as well as being decorative in its own right. Select the elements with care and reject anything that does not look right, no matter how much you like it. However, not everything has to match, there is a real mixture of stuff in this picture, but the overall look is stunning and one hundred per cent successful. The tortoiseshell and silver boxes and the magnificent blotter and stationary box all sit happily together, though they are not a set. The family photos in slim metal frames are a deeply personal touch and they blend with the other silver ornaments.

Towering over all of these things is an elegant vase holding a very natural display of flowers. The straight sides and narrow mouth make it an extremely easy vase in which to create a display at speed (when you have to pick flowers from the garden, in between showers of rain, just before your guests arrive). The green and white look very fresh against both the silver and the glass, and the classic roses complement the whole display. Placing flowers in front of a mirror doubles both their size and reflects their beauty in every sense of the word. The Chinese lamp, with its toning ivory silk pleated shade, is another essential element. When switched on at night it will throw a beautiful soft light over everything around it.

It really is worth keeping one of those brilliant silver cleaning cloths in a drawer close to where silver is displayed. Therefore, if just before your guests arrive you notice that silver is a bit dull or tarnished, it only takes a minute to whip out the cloth and make everything look good again.

THE Pink BEDROOM

S oft pinks and greens, a classic floral chintz and the crispest white bed linen make this bedroom wonderfully feminine and romantic. Smocking is especially pretty in a bedroom, although in masculine colours it can be very stylish in a reception room as well. Choosing a smocking embroidery skein exactly the same colour as the diagonal, padded curtain border has a beautiful effect here, though the skein could also have been matched to a colour picked out of the main fabric design.

This window treatment has a perfect balance, with the tiebacks smocked in the same pattern as the pelmet. It is this attention to detail like this that really unites a window treatment, and indeed a whole room.

The fine horizontally striped fabric lends itself to the gathered valance as well as it does to the upholstered, pleated headboard. The pink stripe is also an excellent match for the pink in the chintz curtains. The appliquéd bed linen, again in those perfect colours, gives the ideal finishing touch to such a pretty

bedroom. It is, in fact, this appliquéd linen that pulls the whole room together, due to both its solid colours and the strong, geometric design. This is especially successful since, as this is a bedroom, the bed is the focal point.

Pleated Headboard

This is a major project in terms of the time and space needed to complete it.
However, the result is brilliant and looks completely professional. These headboards
are terribly expensive to have made but it is easy to produce one yourself –
just follow the instructions carefully and you won't go wrong.

MATERIALS

Paper

*Chipboard (1.5cm- [⁵⁄₈in-] thick
for single and double beds, 2cm-
[³⁄₄in-] thick for kingsize beds)*

*Surform plane (from any good
DIY shop)*

*5cm- (2in-) thick fire resistant
soft foam*

Hammer

*Headboard fittings and legs
(from any good DIY shop, or use
the fittings and legs from an
old headboard)*

Spray glue

Staple gun

*50g (2oz) and 100g (4oz)
wadding, 68cm (27in) wide*

Main fabric

Piping cord

PVA glue

Backtacking strip or thick card

Small tacks

Lining

Screwdriver

MEASURING

*A headboard can be made almost
any shape. Copy the shape of an
existing headboard that you like or
use the proportions, given below, of
the single headboard we made.*

Height: *90cm (35in) (15cm [6in]
of this will be below the level of the
mattress).*

Width: *width of the bed plus
5cm (2in) (this includes 10cm
[4in] border).*

CUTTING THE MATERIALS

Chipboard: *the size of the headboard.*

Foam: *the size of the headboard
minus the border around the top
and side edges, minus 15cm (6in) at
the bottom edge.*

50g (2oz) wadding: *one piece
2.5cm (1in) larger all round than
the foam. One piece 15cm (6in) by
the width of the headboard.*

100g (4oz) wadding: *enough rolled
1m (39in) lengths to run round the
border, butted end to end.*

Main fabric – centre: *5cm (2in)
larger all round than the 50g (2oz)
wadding.*

Main fabric – border: *three
times the length of the border by
25cm (10in).*

Main fabric – mattress overlap:
*23cm (9in) by the width of
headboard plus 10cm (4in).*

Main fabric – piping: *5cm (2in)
by the inner and the outer lengths
of the border.*

Piping cord: *twice the length of
the piping.*

Backtacking strip or thick card:
the width of the headboard.

Lining: *10cm (4in) larger than the
headboard.*

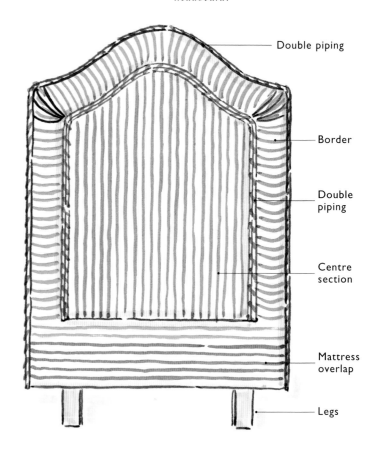

Double piping

Border

Double
piping

Centre
section

Mattress
overlap

Legs

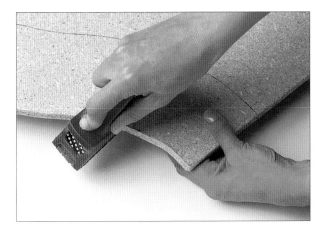

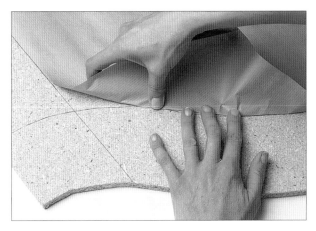

1 Make a paper template the shape and size you want the headboard to be. Cut out the headboard shape from the piece of chipboard. This can be done with a jigsaw, or you can ask the timber merchant you buy the chipboard from to cut it for you. Smooth the edges and corners of the chipboard with the surform plane.

2 In pencil draw a 10cm (4in) border round the sides and top of the chipboard, following the outside shape. Draw a horizontal line across the chipboard 15cm (6in) up from the base (this marks off the mattress overlap). Lay the paper template on the chipboard and crease it along the inner border and mattress overlap lines.

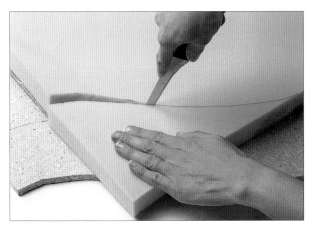

3 Cut out this new paper shape (of the centre section) and draw round it onto the foam in pen. Cut out the shape with a sharp kitchen knife.

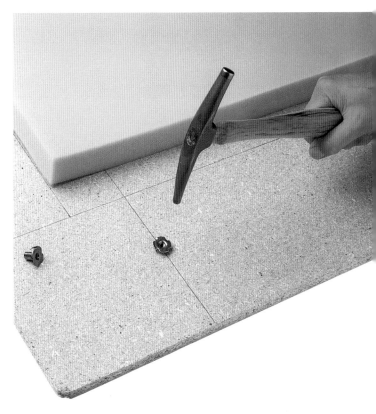

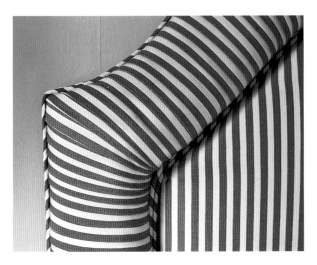

4 Measure from the centre of one screw to the centre of the other on your bed base. Draw a line down the centre of the chipboard. Mark the screw positions on the chipboard, with the centre line as the halfway point. Drill holes for the fixings and hammer them in, with the flat side against the face of the headboard. At this stage, temporarily fit the legs and check that the headboard fits the bed and that its proportions are right.

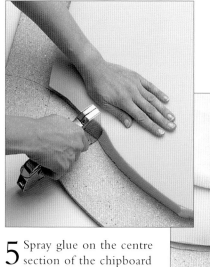

5 Spray glue on the centre section of the chipboard and lay the foam in place; it fits between the pencilled border lines. Press it down firmly. Then, use your left hand to gently push the top edge of the foam backwards and staple into the middle of the thickness every 2.5cm (1in), all round. This pulls the top edge of the foam down and gives a rounded edge.

6 Lay the larger piece of 50g (2oz) wadding over the foam. There is no need to glue it in place.

7 Lay the centre piece of the main fabric over the foam and wadding. Ensure that the wadding and fabric are positioned centrally and then staple the fabric in place. Staple along the base first, then along the top, always working from the middle outwards. Put a few holding staples in first, then you can gently pull the fabric taut as you go. Make small pleats (facing downwards to avoid collecting dust) at the corners.

8 Pleat the strips of fabric for the border with 1cm (½in) pleats. If you are using full widths of fabric, cut off the selvedges before you start. The fabric we are using has a convenient stripe, but on a plain or patterned fabric the pleats should be measured at first, then after a while you will be able to judge the distance by eye. Put a pin in each pleat.

9 Starting at the bottom of one side, lay the first pleated length of fabric right side up on the border section of the headboard, butting a pleated edge up to the foam. The pleats should face downwards on each side of the headboard to avoid collecting dust, so at the centre top of the headboard, make a small box pleat and reverse the direction of the pleats. Staple the pleated fabric to the chipboard with one staple per pleat. To join pleated sections, tuck the raw end of the first section under the first pleat of the new section, so that no raw edges are visible.

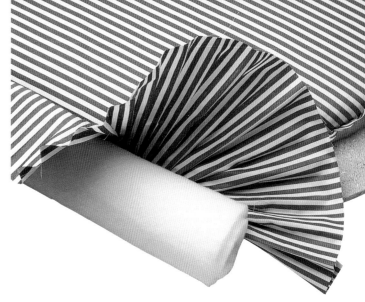

10 At the corners, condense the pleats on the inner edge and fan them out on the outer edge so that they lie flat and evenly around the corners. Make sure that you have enough fabric in the pleats to make an even fan, without losing the pleated look.

11 Roll up 1m (39in) lengths of 100g (4oz) wadding. Starting at the bottom of one side, lay a roll under the pleated fabric. To join rolls invisibly, spray a little glue on the ends and butt up them together. Feather the edges of a small strip of wadding with your fingers, spray on a little glue, and lay it over the join. At the top of the side rolls, following the curved top of the chipboard, cut off the top of the roll, allowing an extra 2.5cm (1in). Lay the first top roll with the end against the side of the board. Trim any projecting ends and fill any gaps with scraps of feathered wadding.

12 Once you have positioned all the wadding rolls, take them off and then, one roll at a time, put them back into position. Check that the pleated section is lying evenly over the roll, then turn the headboard over. Gently pull the pleated fabric taut and then staple it to the back of the chipboard with one staple per pleat. This is the most fiddly bit of the project, so be prepared to take time adjusting the rolls and pleats to achieve a really professional look.

13 When all the rolls are in position and the pleats stapled down, turn the board right side up. Staple the fabric across the ends of the rolls, at the top of the mattress overlap.

14 To make double piping, cut and join 5cm (2in) strips of fabric, using the method shown in steps 7-11 of the *Gathered Valance* (see page 36). Place the first length of piping cord close to one side of the strip, fold the fabric over the cord and machine close to the cord with a zip foot. Machine along the complete required length.

15 Now lay the second length of cord next to the first length, on top of the narrow raw edge. Fold the wide raw edge over the exposed cord, turn the whole thing over and machine along the first line of machining, between the two pieces of cord. Stitch along the complete length of the double piping, then trim any excess fabric close to the line of machining.

16 Run a line of PVA glue down the gap between the centre section and the border of the headboard. Push the inner length of the double piping, raw edge down, into this gap. As you position it, pull gently on the piping to straighten it. Use a gimp pin to anchor the corners.

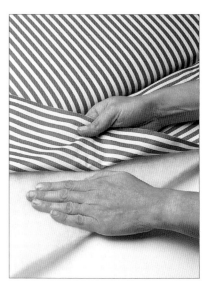

17 At each end of the piping, unpick a few stitches and trim away 1cm (½in) of cord. Staple through this flattened area at each end to anchor it firmly.

18 Right sides facing, lay the mattress overlap strip across the bottom of the board, with one edge on the stapled edge of the centre section. Lay the backtacking strip across this edge and staple it with one staple every 2.5cm (1in), working from the middle outwards.

19 Lay the 15cm (6in) piece of 50g (2oz) wadding across the bottom of the chipboard and fold the overlap strip down over it.

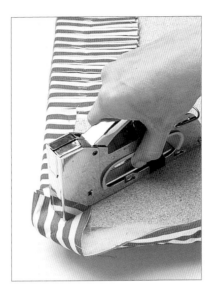

20 Turn the board over and staple the bottom of the overlap to the back of the board.

21 At the corners, pull the point of the fabric over the corner of the chipboard and staple it down. Fold the side and bottom corners over neatly to make a mitre and staple it in place (see above).

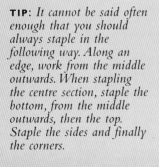

22 Flatten one end of the outer length of piping as in step 17. Tack this end to one of the bottom corners of the headboard with a gimp pin. Place it with the raw end facing towards the top of the headboard, so that when it is doubled back on itself the raw end and the tack are hidden.

TIP: *It cannot be said often enough that you should always staple in the following way. Along an edge, work from the middle outwards. When stapling the centre section, staple the bottom, from the middle outwards, then the top. Staple the sides and finally the corners.*

23 Working in 10-15cm (4-6in) sections at a time, run a line of PVA glue right around the outside edge of the headboard. Glue the double piping in place, pulling it gently to straighten it. Wait for a section to firm up before gluing the next section. On the other side of the headboard, to finish the piping, trim away the cord, turn under the flattened end and tack it in place with a gimp pin.

25 Mark the position of the drilled holes on the lining and screw the legs to the headboard.

24 Lay the headboard face down. Lay the lining over the back of it and, turning the raw edges under a short section at a time, staple it close to the edge all round the headboard.

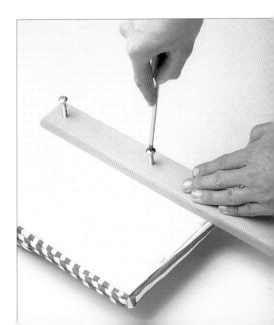

Appliquéd Bed Linen

This bed linen a most original touch and so inviting when the colours tie in with the surroundings. It is an extremely easy project to execute, but do practice the satin stitch first on your sewing machine, using the same appliqué fabric and something similar in weight to the sheet. The hand-embroidery stitches are very simple and quick to do.

MATERIALS

Thin card

Small pieces of fabric

Iron-on adhesive webbing

Plain sheet

Water-soluble pen
(available from good haberdashers)

Embroidery thread

Plain Oxford pillowcase

1 Decide on the shapes you wish to appliqué onto the bed linen and cut appropriate templates out of thin card. We have chosen simple diamond and oval shapes. Draw round the templates onto fabric and cut out the shapes.

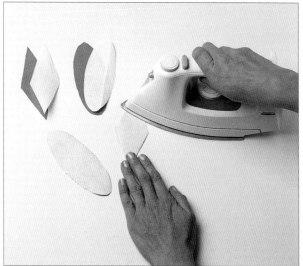

2 Draw and cut out the same shapes in iron-on adhesive webbing. Iron these to the back of the fabric shapes.

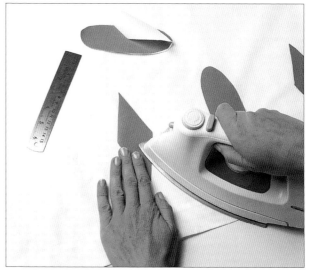

3 Lay the shapes out along the front edge of the top of the sheet. When you are happy with the arrangement, peel off the backing paper of the iron-on adhesive webbing and iron the shapes in place.

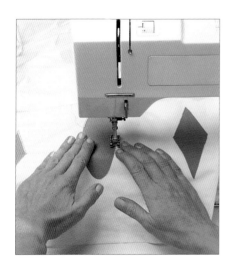

4 Set the sewing machine to satin stitch on the tightest possible setting. You may need to experiment on scraps of fabric to find the best setting for stitching around your chosen shapes. Stitch evenly around each shape, covering the raw edges closely.

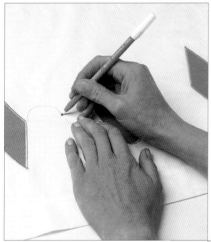

5 Link the diamonds and ovals with an embroidered 'S' shape. Measure the distance between the appliquéd shapes and cut a semi-circular template half the width of this measurement. Put the template beside an appliquéd shape, draw around the top of it in water-soluble pen, then reverse the template and complete the 'S' shape.

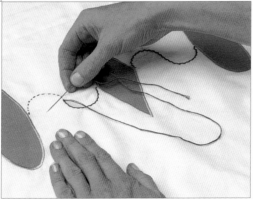

6 To embroider the 'S' in whip stitch, make a line of running stitches, following the drawn line. Then, 'whip' the stitches by taking the needle from right to left under each running stitch in turn. Appliqué the Oxford pillowcase following steps 1–4.

Gathered Valance

This is a fairly major project involving a huge amount of machining. The magic thing is that it is made in such a way that, as with the tablecloth on page 60, all the raw edges are enclosed. It is important that you practise machine pleating before you embark upon this project.

MATERIALS

Main fabric
Lining
Piping cord

MEASURING

Length: *length of the bed.*

Width: *width of the bed.*

Depth: *height from bed base to the floor.*

CUTTING THE FABRICS

Skirt

Main fabric length: *two-and-a-half-times twice the length and once the width of the bed.*

Main fabric depth: *height from the top of the bed base to the floor plus 4cm (1½in) hem, plus 1cm (½in) to 'break' on the floor, plus 3cm (1¼in) seam allowances.*

Lining length: *same as the main fabric.*

Lining depth: *8cm (3in) shorter than the main fabric.*

Bed base and flap

Main fabric – base lip: *two strips 15cm (6in) by the length of the bed plus 5cm (2in). One strip 15cm (6in) by the width of the bed plus 5cm (2in).*

Main fabric – flap: *One strip the width of the bed plus 8cm (3in) by 43cm (17¼in).*

Lining – base length and width: *the size of the top of the bed base plus 1.5cm (⅝in) seam allowances all round.*

Piping: *40cm (16in) square of the main fabric.*

1 Lay out the lining base on a large worksurface or on the floor. Lay the base lip strips, right sides up, on top of the lining base, raw edges aligned. At the corners, the ends of the long sides should lie on top of the ends of the short side.

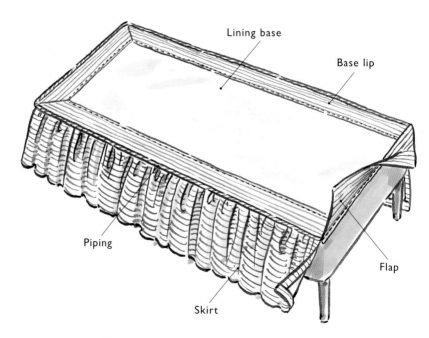

Lining base

Base lip

Piping

Flap

Skirt

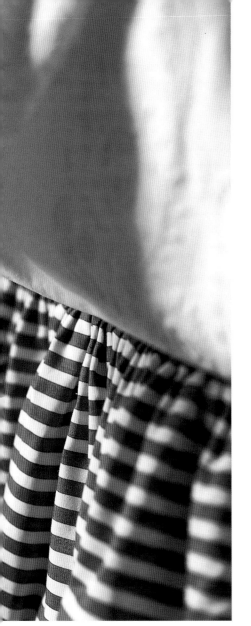

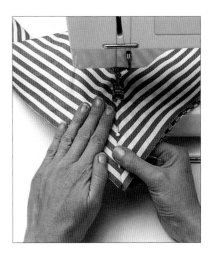

2 Turn under the short edge of one long strip at a 45° angle to make a mitre. Scrape the fold with the metal ruler.

3 Top stitch along the mitre, starting 2cm (¾in) from the inner corner.

4 Machine the skirt lining to the skirt main fabric along bottom edge.

6 Machine the main fabric and the lining together 1cm (½in) from the top edge. With damp fingers, machine gather the top edge to the finished length. To help you judge this, put in a pin every 25cm (10in) along the raw edge. Each 25cm (10in) section must be gathered up to 10cm (4in). Measure the gathered sections as you go and adjust where necessary.

5 Fold the lining and the main fabric in half lengthways, right sides facing, so that top raw edges are aligned. The hem should measure 4cm (1½in): check this with the metal ruler and press.

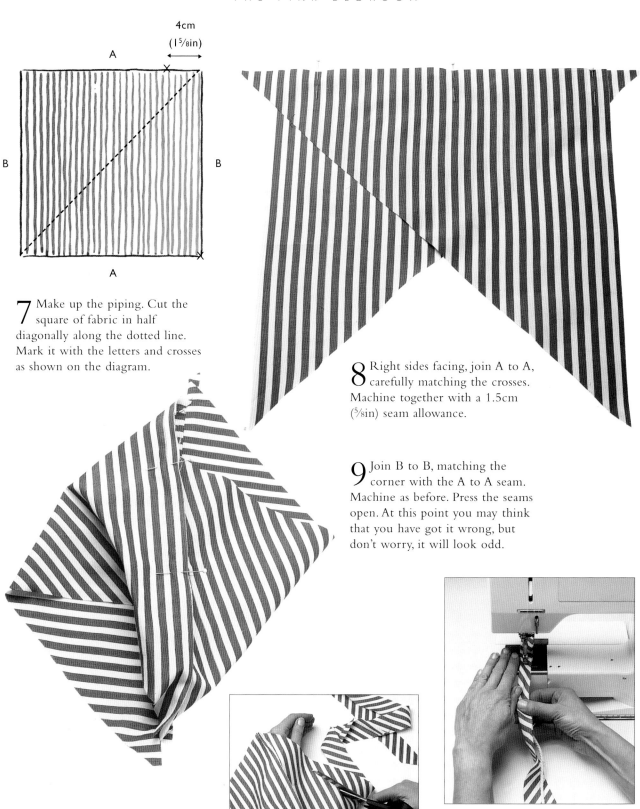

4cm
(1⅝in)

A

B   B

A

7 Make up the piping. Cut the square of fabric in half diagonally along the dotted line. Mark it with the letters and crosses as shown on the diagram.

8 Right sides facing, join A to A, carefully matching the crosses. Machine together with a 1.5cm (⅝in) seam allowance.

9 Join B to B, matching the corner with the A to A seam. Machine as before. Press the seams open. At this point you may think that you have got it wrong, but don't worry, it will look odd.

10 With the wrong side facing out, slip the circle of fabric over your wrist. Cut a 4cm (1½in) continuous strip from the fabric. You will find that you only need to measure occasionally to keep the strip even.

11 Wrong sides facing and raw edges aligned, fold the strip over the piping cord. Machine close to the cord with a zip foot.

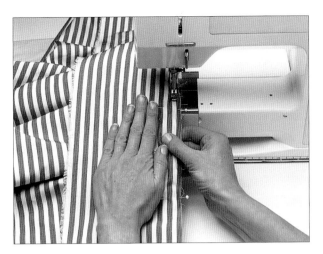

12 Assemble the valance by making the following 'sandwich', with all raw edges aligned. At the bottom, right side down, lay the lining base. On top of this, right side up, lay the skirt. On top of this, lay the piping and on top of that, right side down, lay the base lip. Pin through all layers.

13 Carefully machine the all the layers together. Wrong sides facing, bring the lining base and the base lip together, enclosing all the raw edges.

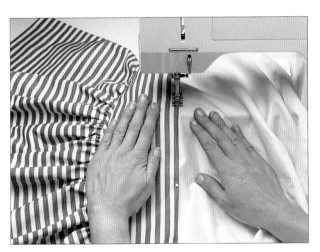

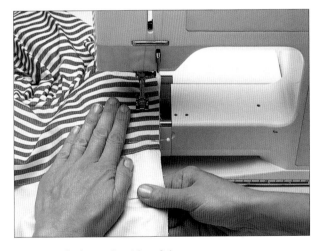

14 Turn under 1.5cm (⅝in) on the inner edge of the base lip and top stitch it to the lining base.

15 With the right side of the flap facing the wrong side of the bed base, machine the flap to the bed base.

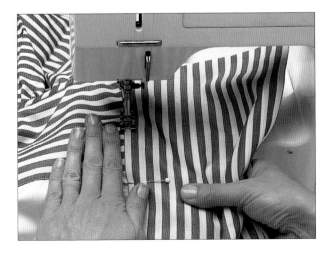

16 Turn under and press 1.5cm (⅝in) along the other long side of the flap. Right sides facing, fold the flap in half lengthways, so that the pressed fold touches the seam sewn in step 15. Machine down both short sides. Turn right side out, so that the open edge of the flap is against the right side of the bed base. Topstitch this folded edge to the bed base.

Curtain with Contrast Leading Edge

The contrast leading edge, which is also lightly padded, is an added detail, done right at the start, that puts this curtain into a league of its own. It is fairly extravagant to cut the leading edge on the cross, but with a striped fabric, so worthwhile for the sophisticated look.

MATERIALS

Main fabric
Contrast fabric
50g (2oz) wadding
Interlining
Lining
Lead weights
Pencil-pleat tape
Curtain hooks

MEASURING

The same as The Classic Curtain (see page 10).

CUTTING FABRICS

For each curtain

Main fabric, lining and interlining: *the same as* The Classic Curtain *(see page 10).*

Contrast fabric: *15cm (6in) by the same length as the main fabric, cut on the cross.*

Wadding: *the same as the contrast fabric, but cut straight.*

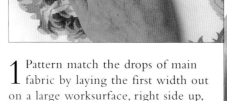

1 Pattern match the drops of main fabric by laying the first width out on a large worksurface, right side up, with one selvedge parallel to a long side of the worksurface and the raw short edge aligned with the top of the worksurface. Clamp the fabric in position. Turn under the selvedge of the second width and line it up with the first width, as closely as possible to the top, so that the pattern matches. Pin the widths together, inserting vertical pins parallel to the turned-under selvedge and matching the pattern carefully. Scrape between the pins with the metal ruler. Then, on the wrong side, pin the widths together with horizontal pins, across the scraped line, in the gaps between the vertical pins, which can then be removed. Machine the widths together, over the pins, following the scraped line exactly.

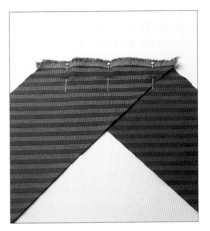

2 Fold the raw end of the contrast fabric over at a 45° angle to align with one selvedge. Cut along the fold.

3 Mark and cut on the cross 15cm (6in) strips of the contrast fabric.

4 Pin the ends of the strips together as shown. Note that the corners overlap by the depth of the seam allowance so that when the strip is machined and opened out, the joins are straight. If the corners are matched exactly, the joins will be stepped.

5 Machine the strips together to achieve the required length. Press the seams open.

6 Right sides facing, lay a strip of the contrast fabric along the leading edge of the main fabric. Lay the wadding on top of the contrast fabric. Pin the layers together and turn the fabrics over; they must be machined from the fabric side as the wadding will catch in the foot of the sewing machine. Machine the three layers together, taking a 4cm (1½in) seam allowance.

7 Lay the main fabric right side down, with the contrast folded out and the wadding folded in half. Lay the interlining over the main fabric and wadding and interlock it to the contrast edge, just beyond the wadding. Make rows of interlocking stitches 40cm (16in) apart across the curtain, starting and stopping 20cm (8in) from the top and bottom.

Make up the curtain as described in steps 6–21 of *The Classic Curtain* (see page 10).

Smocked Pelmet

This looks so time-consuming and complicated, but it isn't. You can smock almost anywhere, with the work in your lap, and it must be one of the most therapeutic and creative pastimes. However, never attempt to cover this quantity of tiny buttons – it will drive you mad. Send the fabric to a button-covering service, it will make your job much easier.

MATERIALS

Main fabric

Contrast fabric

Fan-edge trim

Interlining

Lining

Covered buttons (see Suppliers on page 126)

Embroidery thread

MEASURING

The same as Banded Pelmet with Soft Skirt *(page 16)*

CUTTING THE FABRICS

Main fabric length: *drop of the pelmet plus 8.5cm (3¼in).*

Main fabric width: *two times the width of the finished pelmet plus 5cm (2in) seam allowances.*

Contrast fabric: *7cm (2¾in) by the same width as the main fabric.*

Fan-edge trim: *4cm (1½in) longer than the width of the pelmet.*

Interlining length: *8cm (3in) shorter than the main fabric.*

Interlining width: *5cm (2in) narrower than the main fabric.*

Lining length: *12cm (4¾in) shorter than the main fabric.*

Lining width: *the same as the main fabric.*

Covered buttons: *Approximately 56 for each width of fabric.*

Embroidery thread: *Approximately 1¾ skeins for each width of fabric.*

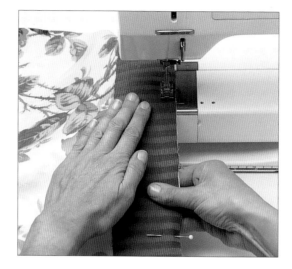

1 Right sides facing and raw edges aligned, machine the contrast strip to the top edge of the main fabric.

2 Press the contrast strip out flat, seam allowances towards the top.

3 Turn up and press 7cm (2¾in) along bottom edge of the main fabric. Leaving 1cm (½in) free beyond the edge of the main fabric, machine the fan-edge trim to the fabric, with the bottom of the webbing level with the pressed line. Right sides facing, machine the lining to the bottom edge of the main fabric, starting and stopping 11cm (4½in) from the side edges.

4 Lay the pelmet face down and lay the interlining on top of it. The top edge should be level with the top edge of the main fabric and the bottom edge level with the pressed line.

5 Turn down the contrast strip so 1.5cm (⅝in) is visible on the right side. Press firmly.

Make up the pelmet as described in steps 6-9 of *Banded Pelmet with Soft Skirt* (see page 16). Machine on and pull up pencil-pleat tape as described in steps 20-21 of *The Classic Curtain* (see page 10). Machine the tape at the top close to the highest cord (be careful not to catch the cord in the machining), and as close to the lower edge as possible at the bottom.

6 First smock the top row, working just below the contrast band. Thread your needle with embroidery thread. Working from left to right across the curtain, pinch the first two pleats together. Bring the needle to the front, just to the left of the pleats, then pass it through the pleats from right to left. Thread a button onto your needle and take the needle to the back through the right-hand hole, then move on to the next pair of pleats. Passing the needle along at the back of the curtain, repeat the sequence on each subsequent pair of pleats. Smock the bottom row in exactly the same way, following the line of machining at the bottom of the tape.

7 Measure, and mark with a water soluble pen, the next row, which lies on the halfway point between the two rows of buttons. With practise, you will be able to judge this point by eye, without having to measure and mark. Smock this row in the same way, but working on alternate pairs of pleats to those smocked in rows one and three. The buttons on row two sit between those of rows one and three, both horizontally and vertically.

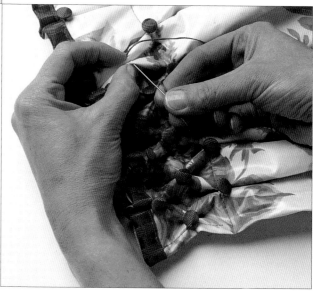

8 Outline the smocking with embroidery thread wound round the buttons. First work from left to right along rows one and two. Tie the end of the skein of thread firmly around the base of the button furthest to the left on the middle row. Trim the end. Wind the thread anticlockwise around the next button along on the top row. Bring the thread down to the next button along, on the middle row, and wind it around clockwise. Continue along the top of the pelmet in this way. When you reach the end, work back along from right to left going anticlockwise around the buttons on row three and clockwise, again, around the buttons on row two.

FLORALS, STRIPES AND CHECKS

Pink is frequently used in a bedroom because it so easy to be successful with it. Varying shades of pink, white, cream, blue and green blend beautifully together. The slightly faded 'English rose' look is always lovely and is quite successful on its own. However, it is much more interesting to introduce some fresh stripes, checks, embroidered or textured fabrics to dilute the flowers. This can pull the room together and energise the flowers. Equally, such an arrangement also works the other way round: checks, stripes and solid colours can be softened and made more feminine when used with floral prints.

1 *Leclair – Russet.*

2 *Chintz from a selection by Warners.*

3 *Windemere – Cerise.*

4 *Britain – Cerise.*

5 *Athelier – Strawberry*

6 *Littlefield – Cerise.*

7 *Tabella – Cerise.*

8 *Versaille Rose E7351.*

FABRIC CHIC

Smocked Tieback

The smocking pattern on the pelmet is reflected in this tieback. The clever thing is to insert the tape between the two pieces of chintz so that it is completely hidden.

MATERIALS

Main fabric

Interlining

Pencil-pleat tape

Contrast fabric

Buttons

Embroidery thread

MEASURING

As for Plaited Tieback with Rosette *(see page 20)*

CUTTING THE FABRICS

For each tieback

Tieback length: *two pieces double the measured length plus 3cm (1¼in) seam allowances.*

Tieback width: *the width of the pencil-pleat tape plus 3cm (1¼in).*

Interlining and pencil-pleat tape length: *3cm (1¼in) shorter than the main fabric.*

Interlining width: *the width of the pencil-pleat tape.*

Contrast fabric: *6cm (2½in) by circumference of tieback plus 3cm (1¼in).*

1 Curve the corners of both the pieces of main fabric. Make a 'sandwich' of a piece of the main fabric, right side down, a strip of interlining, a length of pencil-pleat tape and the second piece of main fabric, right side up. Tie together the cords at one end of the tape. Make sure the other ends are 5cm (2in) long and leave them free. Make a tiny hole 2.5cm (1in) from one end of the tieback and feed the free ends of the cord through it.

2 Machine right round the tieback taking a 1.5cm (⅝in) seam allowance. Make sure that you do not catch the free ends of the cords in the machining.

TIP: *If you have a fabric with a relatively large pattern repeat, as we have here, tiebacks are the perfect way to use up the offcuts, which can otherwise be wasted. If the tieback is flat and the pattern very pronounced, both tiebacks should be cut from the same part of the pattern or they will visually 'jar' when the window treatment is hung. However, with this style of tieback the smocking distorts the pattern, so the tiebacks can be cut from any scrap pieces.*

3 The free ends of the cord should be on the outside of the tieback as shown.

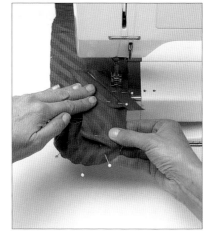

4 Right side down, pin the contrast strip right around the back of the tieback. Machine it in place using a small stitch and with a 1.5cm (⅝in) seam allowance. Small rucks may appear on the corners, but you can flatten these out with the closed blades of a small pair of scissors.

5 When you reach the join in the contrast fabric, turn the raw ends over and stitch right across them. Be careful not to catch the free ends of the cord in the line of machining.

6 Oversew the ends together with very close, tiny stitches.

8 Pull on the cords to pull the tieback up to the required length. Knot the cords together, cut the ends and push them back through the hole.

Smock and outline the tieback as described in steps 6-8 of *Smocked Pelmet* (page 42).

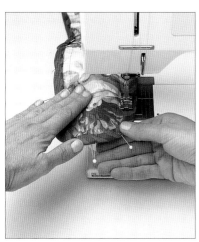

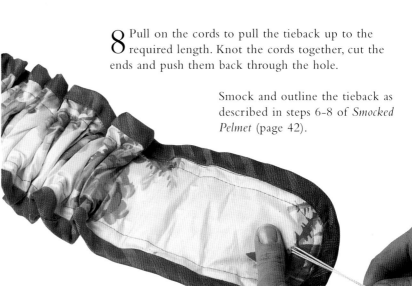

7 Fold the contrast fabric to the right side and turn the raw edge under so that 1.5cm (⅝in) shows at the front. Top stitch right round the tieback, close to the turned-under edge. Make sure you do not catch in the free ends of the cords in the line of machining.

ARRANGING A **DRESSING** TABLE

If you inherit such a thing as a pretty dressing table set, it is lovely to display it, as opposed to keeping it hidden away all the time. To actually make use of it, beyond it being a purely decorative object, is also brilliant. Little pots can be filled with all those essential but untidy items which are good to have accessible – safety pins, needle and thread, cleansing pads, favourite earrings. Airtight silver-topped pots are can successfully be used to store face and cleansing creams. The silver is easy to keep clean by rubbing it once a week with a special cleaning cloth, which you can keep in a drawer below.

Ivory-style objects also look charming on a dressing table, due to their gentle colour, and they blend beautifully with silver, china, glass, mahogany, linen and lace. If you do choose to put a pretty lace or linen cloth down on the surface of your dressing table, it is worth having a piece of 3mm (⅝in) glass, with bevelled edges, cut to fit the table top, then your linen will stay clean.

Candles are so reassuring in case of a power cut or a fuse blowing – quite apart from creating a very soft and romantic light. Flowers are also heavenly things to have in your bedroom; they bring a feeling of peace and freshness, as well as providing a delicious scent.

You cannot have a dressing table without a looking glass and preferably one that is well lit. I love the antique mahogany ones on a stand, with mirrors that you can tilt and little drawers underneath that you can fill with your pretty hankies, favourite beads or special keys. Here, however, a very contemporary mirror blends in well with the antique stuff – an interesting twist to a conventional situation. Paintings on the walls add even more charm and interest to the room and the framed, sentimental photographs add a very personal finishing touch.

THE Country KITCHEN

A country-style family kitchen really is the heart of the home. It is where you all congregate to eat informally, discuss the events of the day, and to warm up by the Rayburn in chilly weather. Therefore, everything should have a home; your kitchen must not be messy as that will make it unwelcoming.

No kitchen is complete without a trellised noticeboard to hold all those pretty postcards and vital bits of information that must not be lost. This one is the most perfect marriage between chenille fabric and jute braid. The blue-and-taupe colour scheme is continued in a traditional fabric tablecloth, which gives the kitchen the cosy and inviting air a plastic cloth doesn't begin to offer. The wide border gives the cloth the most perfect finish, as well as enclosing all the raw edges to prevent fraying.

Making 'frock' covers for very ordinary kitchen chairs smartens them up and helps the room to double up as a dining room (the 'frocks' are removable and so are easy to look after). Dressers give a particularly cosy and homely feel to any kitchen,

as well as looking extremely pretty with china displayed on them. They are also immensely practical as they offer excellent storage space and an extra surface upon which to work.

Chair Covers

This is a challenging project which will take time to do well, but it is worth every minute of the effort involved. The most suitable chairs for this project are straight-backed wooden chairs: if the chair has a padded seat already, then so much the better as you can pin into it when fitting the cover.

MATERIALS

Main fabric
Covered buttons

MEASURING

Measure all the sections of the chair marked in Figure 1

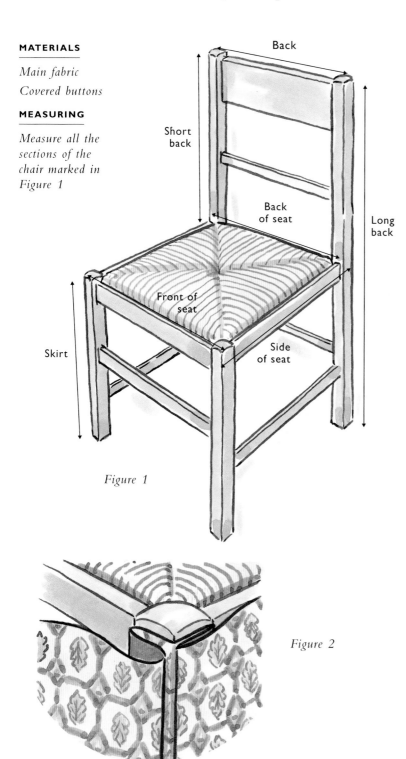

Figure 1

Figure 2

CUTTING THE FABRICS

If you are using a patterned fabric, consider the pattern matching when you are cutting. It may well not be possible to make a perfect match, but you can improve the appearance of the cover enormously by arranging the pieces so that they works harmoniously across the seams (see step 2). To this end, you may find it easiest to make paper templates of the various pieces and pin these to the fabric before cutting.

Seat and short back sections: *measure the front, back and side of the seat and the height of the short back. Cut one of each according to the measurements plus 1.5cm (⁵⁄₈in) seam allowances all round.*

Two long back sections: *measure the length of the long back and half the width of back. Cut two according to the measurements plus 1.5cm (⁵⁄₈in) seam allowances on each long outer side, plus 9cm (3¹⁄₂in) on each inner long side, plus 3cm (1¹⁄₄in) on the hems.*

Skirt length: *measure the height of the skirt. Cut one according to the measurements plus 1.5cm (⁵⁄₈in) seam allowance at the top and 3cm (1¹⁄₄in) at the hem.*

Skirt width: *measure the front and both sides of the seat. Cut one according to the measurements plus 8cm (3in) for each front box pleat. plus 1.5cm (⁵⁄₈in) seam allowance at each end.*

Ties: *six ties, each measuring 4 x 60cm (1¹⁄₂ x 24in).*

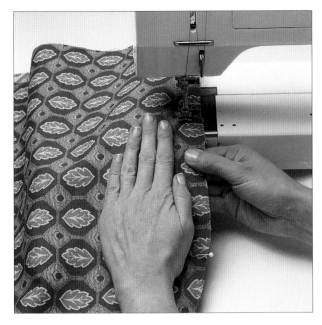

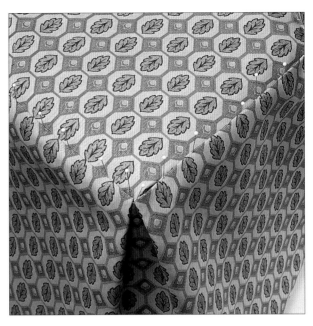

1 Right sides facing, pin seat and short back sections together where they meet at the back of the seat. Check they fit the chair then machine them together.

2 Wrong sides facing, pin the skirt to the seat, folding and positioning the box pleats as shown in Figure 2 (see page 52). Put the cover over the chair and adjust the pins if necessary so that the cover fits neatly. Take the time to do this carefully and accurately.

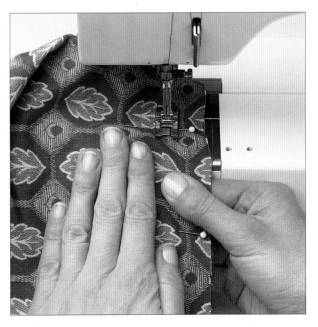

3 Machine the skirt to the seat, starting at the back of one side. Fold the box pleat out of the way and machine right up to the front corner; do a few reverse stitches to finish. Take the fabric off the machine, fold the pleat back in place and machine from the fold to the corner, over the first line of machining. Machine both sides in this way.

4 Along the front seam, fold the unsewn half of each pleat out of the way. Mark the corners with a pin and machine exactly from pin to pin along the front seam.

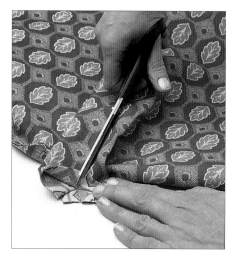

5 Clip into the seam allowance at the centre of each box pleat. Fold the unsewn half of the pleat back into place on the front seam and machine as before.

6 Zigzag the inner edges of the long back sections to to neaten them. Turn under and press a 1cm (½in) hem, then turn under and press a 6cm (2½in) hem.

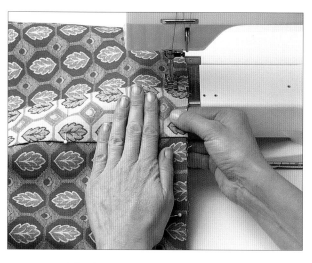

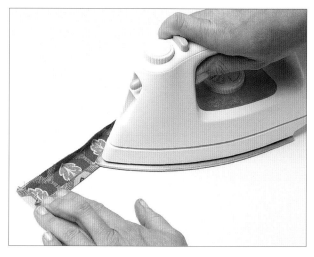

7 Pin and fit the long back sections to the chair cover as before, overlapping the inner edges. Machine the sections to the cover, starting along the top seam.

8 Turn under and press a 0.5cm (¼in) seam on all edges of each tie; turning under the short edges first.

TIP: *If you are making several covers for identical chairs, make one in calico, using large machine stitches. Fit it carefully, trim the side seams to exactly 1cm (⅝in), then take it apart and use it as a pattern for all the proper covers.*

As with any fabric in the kitchen, your chair covers will probably need frequent washing. Therefore, do check the cleaning instructions before you buy a fabric. If you are in any doubt it is worth getting a sample and washing it yourself. There is nothing more depressing than putting a lot of work into a project and then having it completely ruined in the first wash.

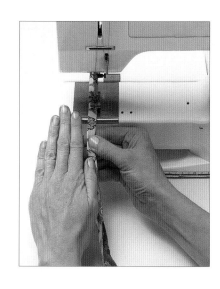

9 Fold each tie in half lengthways and top stitch very close to the turned under edges.

10 Right sides facing, pin the ties to the inner edges of the back of the chair cover in pairs. Each tie should have the long end pointing away from the opening. Space them equally, with the lowest pair about halfway between the seat and the bottom of the cover. Remember that one edge overlaps the other, so the tie on the underside edge needs to be pinned on level with the overlap. Machine each tie in place, stitching in a rectangle across the width and about 2cm (¾in) along the long edges. Fold the tie back on itself and hand-stitch it to the end of the machined section.

Put the cover on the chair and do up the ties. Then turn up and machine a double 1.5cm (⅝in) hem all round the bottom edges.

Buttons can be a pretty alternative to ties. Simply make buttonholes in the overlapping edge and stitch buttons in place on the underside edge. We have covered buttons in the same fabric as the chair, centring the acorn motif in the middle of the button.

Trellised Noticeboard

These noticeboards are an instantly attractive soft furnishing item which are deeply satisfying to make due to the speed of their production, and they make fabulous presents for friends. They require few materials and involve absolutely no sewing – merely a few basic tools.

MATERIALS

1.5cm- (⅝in-) thick chipboard

Hand saw

100g (4oz) wadding

Main fabric (choose a fabric that does not fray too easily)

Staple gun and staples

Braid or strong ribbon (such as grosgrain ribbon)

Decorative upholstery studs

Hammer

Lining material

Two mirror plates

MEASURING

The noticeboard can be made to fit any space: this one measures 50 x 50cm (20 x 20in).

CUTTING THE MATERIALS

Chipboard: *the size of the finished noticeboard.*

Wadding: *2cm (¾in) larger all round than the chipboard.*

Main fabric: *8cm (3in) larger all round than the chipboard.*

Braid: *twice the diagonal measurement of the board from corner to corner, plus four times the diagonal measurement from the central point of one side to the central point of the adjoining side, plus approximately 40cm (16in).*

Lining material: *2.5cm (1in) bigger all round than the chipboard.*

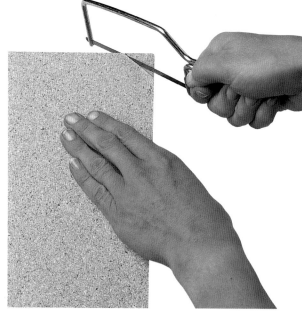

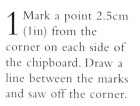 1 Mark a point 2.5cm (1in) from the corner on each side of the chipboard. Draw a line between the marks and saw off the corner.

2 Lay out the piece of wadding and place the chipboard centrally on top of it. Cut off the corners of the wadding.

3 Lay out the main fabric and place the wadding and chipboard centrally on top of it. Starting in the middle of one side, gently pull the fabric over to the back of the chipboard and staple it in place. Staple 1cm ($\frac{1}{2}$in) in from the raw edge of the fabric and work evenly in both directions from the middle towards the corners. Stop stapling 5cm (2in) from each corner. Staple the opposite side in the same way, then the top and bottom edges.

4 Pull the corner of the fabric tightly over the chipboard and staple it in place with two staples. Cut off the point, fold the sides in and staple them in place (see inset).

5 Staple one end of the braid across the centre of one corner of the back of the chipboard. Leave about a 3cm (1in) free end and use two staples to anchor it.

6 Run the braid diagonally across the noticeboard from corner to corner, pulling it firmly, then cutting and stapling the ends, as in step 5. Mark the centre of each side of the noticeboard with a pin. In turn, pin each strip of braid in place on the front of the board, 2.5cm (1in) away from the central pins. Then turn the board over and staple the braid, as in step 5.

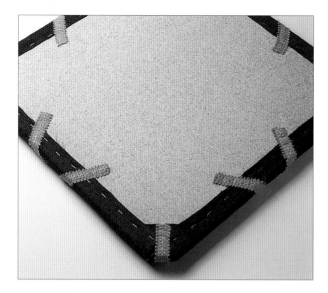

7 The braid must be stapled to the back of the chipboard at an angle, as shown, to allow it to lie smoothly across the front.

8 Hammer in a decorative upholstery stud at each point where the lengths of braid cross on the front of the noticeboard.

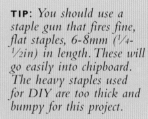

TIP: *You should use a staple gun that fires fine, flat staples, 6-8mm (1/4-1/2in) in length. These will go easily into chipboard. The heavy staples used for DIY are too thick and bumpy for this project.*

When hammering in the studs, hold each stud in position between your fingers (see step 8) and tap it lightly, until it holds. Be careful not to hit your hand. Then remove your fingers and hammer the stud home.

9 Turn under and press, or scrape with a small metal ruler, 3cm (1 1/4in) all round the lining. Lay it centrally on the back of the noticeboard and staple it in place 0.5 cm (1/4in) from the edge. At the corners, turn under the point, keeping the distance between the edge of the noticeboard and the edge of the lining equal, and staple it in place.

10 Position the mirror plates: either place two along the top edge or one in the middle of the top and bottom edges. Use a bradawl to make an initial hole and then screw the mirror plates in place.

BRILLIANT BLUES

People have had blue and white kitchens for years and they look brilliant. But this is something different – these navy and cream or taupe combinations go one step further. They are very sophisticated for a kitchen, and so chic if you want the room to double up for entertaining as well. The cream brings life to the navy, just as the navy brings character to the cream.

Here we are mixing not just checks, stripes and patterns, but also linens, chenilles and heavy weaves. All are highly successful in a room that needs to be very warm and inviting, while remaining smart and sophisticated at the same time.

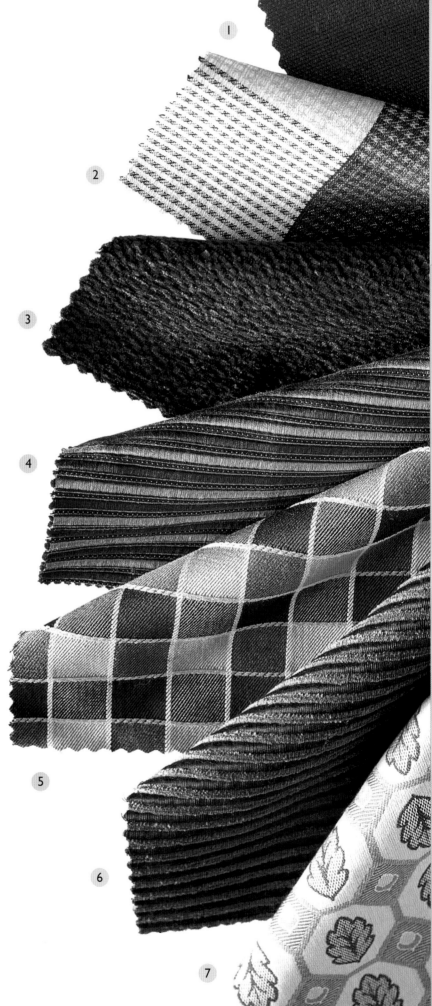

1 *Kerry L1005.*

2 *Dorrance – Royal.*

3 *Barnshaw – Indigo.*

4 *Calamar – Indigo.*

5 *Buckmont – Indigo.*

6 *Hurston – Navy.*

7 *Hampshire – Cobalt.*

Tablecloth
with Wide Border

A big worksurface will help you make this project with ease –
especially as you need to be precise when mitring the corners.
Putting a border on the cloth in this way encloses all
the raw edges, so it will withstand a lot of washing as well as
looking so stylish. To this end, do check the cleaning
instructions before you buy the fabric.

MATERIALS

Main fabric

Border fabric

MEASURING

Width: *the width of the table top
plus half the drop from the tabletop
to the floor on each side.*

Length: *the length of the table top
plus half the drop from the tabletop
to the floor on each side.*

CUTTING THE FABRICS

Main fabric: *the measured size plus
1.5cm (⅝in) all round (if you have
to join widths, add a piece to each
side, pattern matching it, so that the
area covering the tabletop has no
seams in it).*

Border fabric: *two strips the width
of the cloth by 16cm (6¼in) and
two strips the length of the cloth by
16cm (6¼in).*

1 With the right side of the
border facing the wrong side of
the main fabric, machine the
border strips to the main fabric,
aligning the raw edges.

2 Press the border strips
over to the right side
of the main fabric. The
wrong side of the border
should be facing the right
side of the main fabric. Press
over the two side strips first,
followed by the end strips.

3 Fold the border strips out and trim the ends level with the sides of the main fabric. Cut an angle at the corners of each end strip, as shown, to reduce bulk in the corners. Do this carefully so that you do not expose the corner seam. Fold the side strips back in place.

4 Turn both the corners of each end strip over to make a 45° angle and pin.

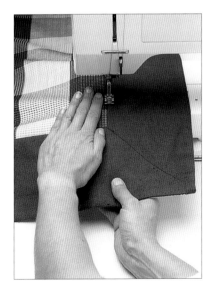

5 Fold the end strip back over the side strip and pin it in place along the angled seam.

6 From the outer edge of the table cloth, measure a 13cm (5in) border. Turn under and press the inner edges of the border.

7 Top stitch each mitred corner and then top stitch the inner edge of the border to the main fabric.

DISPLAYING CHINA ON A **DRESSER**

Dressers are the cleverest of designs; they are so deeply practical and so terribly pretty as a piece of furniture. In a kitchen you can fill them with a huge amount of stuff, which is then not only permanently displayed but is also easily accessible.

Most shelves on a dresser are made with not only a lip on the front to stop things falling off, but also a groove at the back so that your plates can stand up there and look pretty. You can screw hooks onto the front of all the shelves for all those mugs, cups, jugs and gravy boats. Below the shelves you have a large working surface where your chopping board can live. The drawers are deep so masses of tea towels, tablecloths, napkins, cutlery, kitchen utensils, and a first aid kit, can fit into them. Below the worksurface, in the cupboards, endless amounts of large clutter can live, like saucepans and large china dishes. What you can also do is remove the cupboard doors altogether and merely have open shelves, which are even easier to access. It looks extremely attractive if you have baskets fitting these lower shelves exactly, which merely pull in and out. The only down side of this is that you can't stop the dirt and dust getting to the stuff stored there.

Remember that things do not have to match on a dresser; it's the combination of a variety of colours, textures and designs that look so attractive together. Dressers also look terrific in nurseries covered in a books, china ornaments, and toys.

Dressers are nearly always made of pine. The trend over the recent years has been to strip the wood and leave it at that. In actual fact, they were always designed to be painted since years ago pine was regarded as such low-grade wood. A paint effect with some kind of distressed finish, like this one, looks simply brilliant. The dresser will look especially homely when it starts to become a little bit worn around the handles and along the edges.

THE Master BEDROOM

A ny bedroom must be a joy to walk into. You should be surrounded by a variety of pretty stuff, which will, of course, include lots of carefully selected fabrics, in a mixture of colours and weaves, but with one common theme holding the whole room together.

You may not spend much time in your bedroom but it is vital that it is perfect for those peaceful moments. Breakfast in bed should be a treat enhanced by having a relaxing environment to enjoy it in.

We have chosen a green, red, white and cream colour scheme, with lots of plain fabrics to set off the patterned curtains and bedhead (see, *Style Story: Dressing a Bed*, page 74), and the toning checked chair and valance. However, what these plain fabrics lack in pattern, they make up for in texture.

The chenille self-striped bedcover has a lavish air of richness about it, due especially to its sumptuous, ruched border. Its weight makes it a very warm and comforting bedcover to sleep beneath.

The elegant chenille cushions draw your eye to the window seat and successfully break up its horizontal line, apart from also looking extremely pretty. The stylish voile curtain filters the light and gives privacy at the same time.

Bedcover with Ruched Border

It is this ruched and padded border, set against the textured cream fabric, that gives this bedcover such a sumptuous look. You need a surprising amount of green to achieve this detail, but it is so worth it. We decided not to interline the bedcover as the material is so heavy in itself. If you wanted to interline, however, you would do it in exactly the same way as for a curtain (see step 3 of *The Classic Curtain*, page 10), with the interlocking stitches in rows 30cm (12in) apart and starting and stopping 6cm (2½in) from the top and bottom.

MATERIALS

Main fabric

Interlining (optional)

Lining

Dinner plate

Lightweight fabric for the border

50g (2oz) wadding

MEASURING

Length: *the length of the mattress, plus the drop from the mattress to the floor minus 15cm (6in), plus 60cm (24in) extra to cover the pillows.*

Width: *the width of the mattress, plus the drop from the mattress to the floor on both sides minus 30cm (12in).*

CUTTING THE FABRICS

Main fabric, interlining (if used) and lining: *the measured size. Place a full width of the main fabric in the middle of the cover and pattern match half widths to each side. Do not be tempted to seam two widths together down the centre of the bedcover, it will look dreadful.*

Border fabric: *18cm (7in) by three times the length of both long sides and one short side of the main fabric.*

Wadding: *12cm (4¾in) by the length of both long sides and one short side. (Overlap strips by 1cm (½in) and zigzag on the machine to join them together.)*

1 Right side facing, machine the lining to the main fabric along the top edge. Press seam open and fold the main fabric back over the lining. Wrong sides facing, machine the main fabric to the lining round all three open sides, very close to the raw edges. Stop 10cm (4in) from each of the bottom corners.

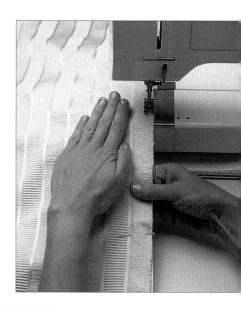

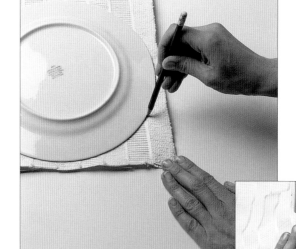

2 Place a dinner plate in each bottom corner and draw round it lightly with a pencil to make a rounded corner. Cut the main fabric and lining along the pencil line and machine them together, as in step 1 (see inset).

3 Working 3cm (1¼in) in from the edge (to provide enough fabric for your right hand to hold), ruche the border strip on the machine by pinching up small 1cm (½in) pleats and catching them in the machining. You will find that dampening your fingers will prevent the fabric slipping.

4 Ruche the other side of the border strip in the same way, working 3cm (1¼in) in from the edge. The pleats must lie in the same direction as those on the other side of the strip, so you must work with the bulk of the fabric to the right in the machine.

5 Right sides facing, lay the ruched border 3cm (1¼in) from the edge of the main fabric and machine the two together, stitching 1mm (¹⁄₁₆in) inside the line of machining holding the ruching in place.

6 Fold the strip of wadding in half and pin it to the top of the cover, aligning the raw edges with the raw edge of the main fabric.

7 Fold the ruched border over the wadding and turn the cover over. Turn the edge of the border over along the line of machining and pin it to the lining, using the pins that were holding the wadding in place. At the corners you will need to cut the line of machining and pull the ruche out so that it lies neatly around the corner.

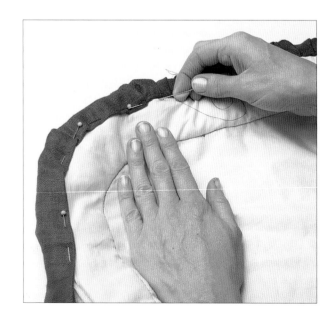

8 Slip stitch the border to the lining all round the border.

Buttoned Cushion

These are easy to make since they require no piping and happily combine a balanced amount of machine and hand sewing. The enormous eye-catching buttons in the centre are so simple to cover and attach.

MATERIALS

Fabric

Cushion pad

Self-cover button kit with two large buttons

Cord

MEASURING

The size of the cushion pad.

CUTTING THE MATERIALS

Fabric: *two pieces the measured size.*

Self-cover buttons: *according to the kit instructions.*

Cord: *the circumference of the cushion pad plus 8cm (3in).*

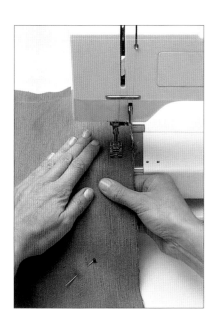

1 Right sides facing, raw edges aligned and starting 10cm (4in) from one corner, machine the pieces of fabric together. Machine up to the first corner, around three sides and 10cm (4in) along from the last corner. Cut off the points of the corners and turn the cover right side out.

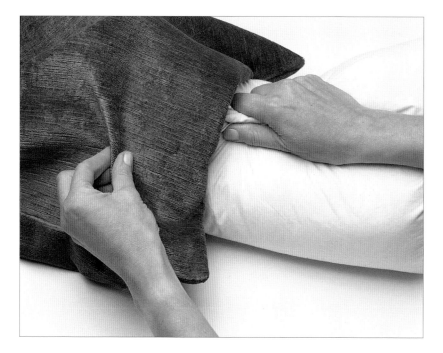

2 Fold the cushion pad in half and stuff it through the opening. Make sure the corners of the pad are snugly inside the corners of the cover then slip stitch the opening closed, leaving a 2.5cm (1in) gap at one end.

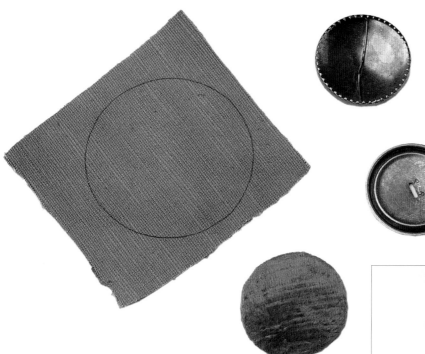

3 Cover the two large buttons according to the kit instructions.

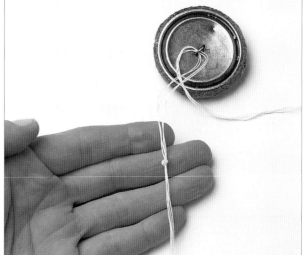

4 Cut a long length of strong button thread. Double the thread, thread it through a sharp, large-eyed needle and double it again. Knot the end. Take the needle through the loop of the button and then through the loop of thread, thus anchoring the thread to the button.

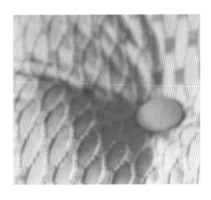

5 Push the needle, which is now attached to one button, right through the centre of the cushion and pull the thread tight. Take the needle through the loop of the second button and back down through the cushion.

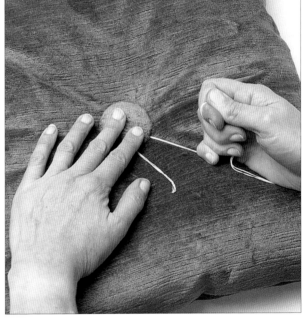

6 Pull the thread very tight, using your left hand to push the button down into the cushion. Wind the end of the thread around and through the button loop, then thread it through itself to anchor it. Do this three times so the buttons are firmly secured.

7 Push one end of the cord into the gap in the cushion. Stitch the cord to the cushion seam all round, catching the underside of the cord with each stitch. Push the other end of the cord into the gap and stitch it firmly closed, catching the cord in the stitches.

TIP: *An alternative to finishing the cord on this cushion is to butt the ends up together and then bind them with an identical-coloured fine fabric, such as a scrap of silk.*

Cushions can be trimmed with almost anything and can be as lavish or as simple as you wish. The only difference comes in when you apply the trimming. Piping, bullion fringes or fan-edge trims need to be inset before the cushion is machined together, while braids and tassels can be stitched on afterwards.

Simple Sheer Curtain

There are many beautiful voiles available on the market that can help make your sheer a very pretty second or third dimension of the overall window treatment, or a successful entity on its own. You can literally cut, sew and hang this item in a matter of minutes rather than hours.

MATERIALS

Voile

Brass drop rod

Two brass cup hooks

MEASURING

Length: *from the top of the architrave to the floor.*

Width: *the length of the pole.*

CUTTING THE FABRIC

Length: *the measured length plus 5cm (2in) for the hem. Add the diameter of the rod doubled, plus 0.5cm (¼in) for the heading (a total of 5cm (2in) in this instance).*

Width: *One-and-a half times the length of the rod.*

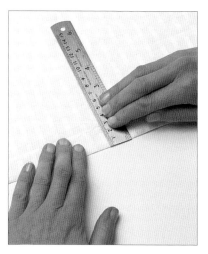

1 At the hem, measure, turn up and pin a 2.5cm (1in) hem.

2 With the end of a metal ruler, scrape along the folded edge to crease the fabric. Turn up another 2.5cm (1in) and scrape again.

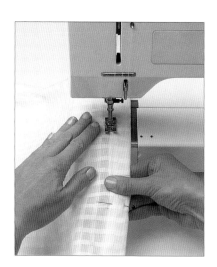

3 Machine very close to the folded edge. Repeat for the heading, turning under half the total heading measurement each time. If the sides of the curtain are selvedges, then leave them as they are. If they are raw, then seal them with a line of zig-zag stitches.

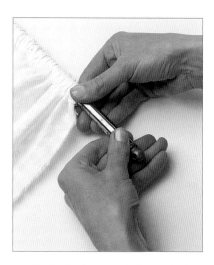

4 Push the brass rod through the heading, pulling the fabric into even gathers along the rod. Screw a brass cup hook into the recess at each side of the window and hang the rod on them.

1   2   3   4

PERFECTLY PLAIN

When you have a very busy print in a room, such as flowers, foliage or swirling creepers, it can be delightfully toned down with some perfectly plain colours. In this way you can also take advantage of another dimension, which is texture.

By using these highly textured weaves, chenilles and linens in a bedroom, you can create an inviting atmosphere with a strong contemporary feel. Patterned fabrics in the room are given visual space and the eye does not become confused or overburdened. So, having used a floral chintz for the curtains, you can then have fun using plain-coloured textured fabrics for items such as cushions and covers. Cushions in chenille are utterly irresistible – you can't help touching and stroking them, and they demand that you relax among them.

1   *Nash C5292.*

2   *Ranjana S1085.*

3   *Kensington V6017.*

4   *Flintshire C5050.*

5   *Riverport C5131.*

6   *Kensington V6016.*

7   *Daventry C5030.*

8   *Paolo L1216.*

5   6   7   8

DRESSING A **BED**

STYLE STORY

A bed should look fresh, comfortable and so inviting. The best way to achieve this is to make the bed up with layers of coverings, which stop it looking large and boring. If you have a really beautiful duvet cover, you do not need a bedcover at all. However, bedcovers can add to the overall design of the room. You can either buy a fabulous cotton one or you can make one yourself with interlining and a beautiful border (see *Bedcover with Ruched Border*, page 66). If you have the fabric quilted first, it looks wonderful and is then incredibly easy to look after as it never creases.

Always put a rug, in some pretty blending colour, at the foot of the bed for extra warmth. There is nothing worse that being cold at night. Small pillows are lovely to have on a bed to offer extra support to a hand, a limb or a book. These can either be in white embroidered linen or in contrasting colours and textures. If you are an eiderdown and blanket (as opposed to a duvet) person, cover the eiderdown in something very pretty – possibly in your curtain or bed valance fabric. Equally, plain or slubbed silks look utterly beautiful on a bed. Your blankets should be palest cream with all their edges bound in a satin ribbon. Then for pure extravagance and elegance, put a blanket cover over the blanket, under the eiderdown, made from an extremely pretty voile. All beds, unless they have stylish legs designed to be exposed, should have a valance for added prettiness.

From a practical point of view, the mattress must be in excellent condition and you must have a headboard for the comfort of reading in bed. As a hostess, you should always sleep in your spare bed to check the following vital things: the comfort of the mattress; the size of the bed for one and for two; the accessibility of the bedside light and a place to put a large bedcover, at night, without cluttering up the room.

I have to say that my biggest concern always is how to keep badly behaved dogs with muddy paws off my beautiful beds.

THE Drawing ROOM

A formal drawing room can be a difficult room to decorate. You want it to look very smart and stylish, but not at all forbidding. If your guests feel uncomfortable in the room they will certainly not be able to relax and enjoy themselves. An brilliant way to make a room inviting is by using strong colour. A big room can be very colourful without looking brash or overpowering, so don't be afraid to be bold with colour.

It is so successful when you produce a number of things for a room, all out of different fabrics, yet all in a complementary or colour scheme. Here the emphasis is not just on colour but also on texture. Embroidered and woven fabrics add an extra element that makes for hugely interesting soft furnishings, which catch your eye as soon as you walk into the room.

Screens are such clever things, used either to break up a room, to conceal a doorway, to cover up untidy items in a corner, or purely as a decorative element in themselves. Apart from looking good, a bolster cushion adds wonderful comfort to a chair or sofa. The grosgrain ribbon rosettes are a feast for the eye, adding a high-relief to the plain lampshade, and the perfectly co-ordinated key tassel is a lovely extra touch.

The Classic Bolster

This bolster is easy to make and fit and the chenille trimming is wonderfully quick and forgiving to inset. The large button at each end gives the bolster a tailored and slightly formal look, while the alternative finish, the tassel, is more frivolous. Also, you can experiment with gathered or pleated ends to see which you prefer.

MATERIALS

Fabric

Flanged trimming

Bolster pad

Self-cover button kit with two large buttons, or two tassels on cord loops

MEASURING

The size of the bolster pad.

CUTTING THE MATERIALS

Main section length: *the length of the pad plus 1cm (½in).*

Main section width: *circumference of the pad plus 1cm (½in).*

Each end strip length: *half the diameter of the pad plus 2.5cm (1in).*

Each end strip width: *the same as the main section.*

Trimming length: *the circumference of the pad twice plus 3cm (1¼in).*

Self-cover buttons: *according to the kit instructions.*

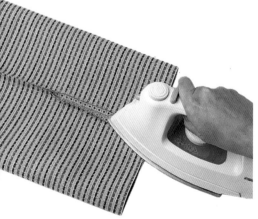

1 Right sides facing, machine up 15cm (6in) at each end of the long edge of the bolster, reversing a few stitches to finish. Press the seam open.

2 Right side up and taking a 1cm (½in) seam allowance, machine the flanged trimming around each end of the fabric tube. Use a zipper foot to help you stitch very close to the edge of the trimming, and start at the seam with 1.5cm (⅝in) of the trimming free. When you have machined all round, turn the cut ends of the trimming away from the fabric and neaten them.

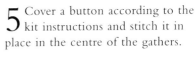

5 Cover a button according to the kit instructions and stitch it in place in the centre of the gathers.

3 Right sides facing, machine the end strips to the main fabric, enclosing the trimming. Use the zipper foot to help you stitch very close to the trimming, and catch in the raw ends. Align the seams in the ends with the seam in the main section and hand-stitch them closed.

4 Turn the cover right side out and insert the pad through the gap in the long seam. Hand-stitch the gap closed. With strong thread, run a line of gathering stitches around each end, 1.5cm (⅝in) from the edge. Pull the gathers up tightly and make a few stitches to finish.

6 Alternatively, you can pleat the end strip. Fold the fabric into pleats and pin them, adjusting the pins until the pleats are even. Catch the pleats in place with tiny stitches 1.5cm (⅝in) from the raw edge.

7 To stitch a button over a pleated end, just follow step 5. Alternatively, a tassel works well on pleats. Stitch the top of the tassel to the centre of the pleats then wind the cord loop around the tassel top, covering the raw edges of the fabric, and stitch it in place as you go.

TIP: *A tassel is a less formal alternative to a button for the end of a bolster.*

Gothic Screen

You need a big space and a table to make this project, and a workbench is helpful but not essential. While there is no sewing involved, this is not a quick project to make but it is worth every staple. With a methodical approach it is terribly easy to achieve a completely professional look.

MATERIALS

Screen blank, or you can re-cover an old screen

Screwdriver

50g (2oz) wadding

PVA glue

Fabric

Staplegun

Pin hammer

Braid

Panel pins

MEASURING

The height and width of one panel of the screen.

CUTTING THE MATERIALS

Cut one piece of fabric and wadding for each side of each panel and one length of braid for each panel.

If you are using a patterned fabric, match the pattern so that it appears in the same way on each side of each panel.

Fabric width: *width of the panel plus 4cm (1½in).*

Fabric length: *length of the panel plus 4cm (1½in).*

Wadding width: *the width of the panel.*

Wadding length: the *length of the panel.*

Braid: *the outside measurement of the panel.*

1 Working on one panel of the screen at a time, take out the hinges. Lay the wadding over one side of the panel, then cut it round the panel so it fits exactly.

2 Squeeze glue onto the panel and smooth the wadding over it.

3 Lay the fabric centrally over the panel. Staple of the fabric, working about 0.5cm (¼in) in from the raw edge, into the middle of the edge of the panel. Put in one staple every 10cm (4in), gently smoothing the fabric as you go.

80

5 At the corners, pinch the fabric to a point and fold it neatly up along one side of the panel (not along the bottom as the extra bulk will make the screen wobbly). Staple the fold in place.

6 Trim away any excess fabric, including the fabric around the shaped top. The raw edge should lie within the width of the edge of the panel.

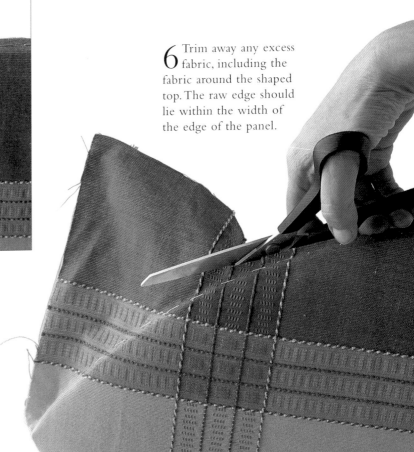

4 Once the fabric is evenly stapled in place all round the panel, go back to the beginning and put in more staples to hold the fabric firmly. The staples should be nearly touching each other.

8 Mark the centre hole of each hinge with a pin, so that you can find it again once the braid has been applied. At the bottom, attach the end of the braid to the side of the panel with a panel pin. Squeeze a 20cm (8in) line of glue along the side and lay the braid over it. Anchor the end of this section of braid with a panel pin, which should be removed once the glue has completely dried. Continue gluing braid around the panel in this way, working in 20cm (8in) stretches.

7 Firmly tap all the staples with the hammer so that they lie completely flat. Turn the screen over and repeat steps 1–7.

9 Screw the hinge back in place in the side of the panel. Do not re-drill a hole as you will damage the fabric and braid and may split the wood. Cover the other panels of the screen following steps 1–9.

TRIMMINGS

Trimmings are the icing on the cake and the utterly delicious
icing at that. They add a vital finishing touch to the success of
any soft furnishing. When there is an opportunity to use a trimming,
not to take it would be a crime and a highly regrettable economy. A
self-made chintz pleat or gather is highly effective. A fine wool, linen,
cotton or silk fan edge gives such a soft and pretty finish, while bullion
has a powerful character of its own and sends a wonderfully strong
statement. Pick the best trimmings you can afford; the choice is huge.

1   *Cotton fringing.*

2   *Frilled edging.*

3   *Jute braid.*

4   *Furnishing cord.*

5   *Jute fringing.*

6   *Grosgrain ribbon.*

7   *Woollen fringing.*

8   *Bullion fringing.*

*This is just a selection of
the types of trimmings
available from most
department stores and
haberdashers shops.*

Rosette Lampshade

This is such an original way to dress up a plain lampshade and
make it into something special. The rosettes are hugely fun and easy to make
and can be done in your lap – so convenient.

MATERIALS

Plain lampshade

*Six lengths of 2.5cm- (1in-) wide
grosgrain ribbon the depth of the
lampshade plus 3cm (1¼in)*

*Six 20cm (8in) lengths of the same
2.5cm- (1in-) wide grosgrain ribbon*

*Six 10cm (4in) lengths of 1.5cm-
(⅝in-) wide grosgrain ribbon in a
different colour*

Six buttons with loops

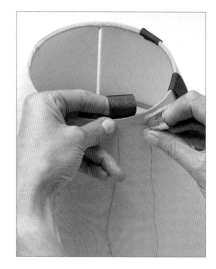

1 Space the first lengths of wide
ribbon equally around the top
of the lampshade and mark their
positions very lightly in pencil.
Hold 1.5cm (⅝in) of one end of a
length in position at the back of
the top of the lampshade and stitch
through the lampshade and the
ribbon, anchoring the ribbon in
place. You will find that a thimble
will help you push the needle
through the lampshade. If the
ribbon frays easily, dab a little PVA
glue on the ends to seal them.
Stitch all six lengths of ribbon to
the shade in this way.

2 Make a line of gathering stitches along one side of
a 20cm (8in) length of 2.5cm (1in) wide ribbon
and pull it up very tightly. On the wrong side, stitch
the short ends together to form a rosette. Do the same
with a 10cm (4in) length of 1.5cm (⅝in) wide ribbon.

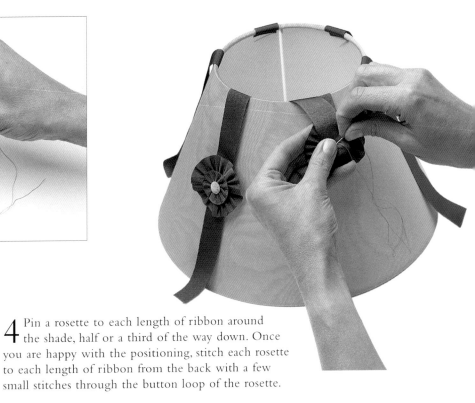

3 Lay the small rosette over the large one and, from the back, stitch the two together with a few small stitches close to the centre. Put the button in the centre of the rosette, pushing the loop through to the back, and stitch through the loop from the back. Make six rosettes in this way.

4 Pin a rosette to each length of ribbon around the shade, half or a third of the way down. Once you are happy with the positioning, stitch each rosette to each length of ribbon from the back with a few small stitches through the button loop of the rosette.

5 Pull each length of ribbon firmly down the shade, making sure it is straight, and fold the raw end to the back. If the end frays, dab it with PVA glue to seal it. With two tiny stab stitches (see page 125), stitch the end of the ribbon in place.

Arabian Tassel

Making your own tassels ensures that you can exactly match your furnishings, both in colour combinations and style. Use them as a stylish key tassel or to decorate cushions 0r headboards; almost anything in fact.

MATERIALS

3cm (1¼in) paper ball

Crochet needle or meat skewer

Two skeins each of two colours of stranded embroidery cotton

Needle

3 x 5cm (1¼ x 2in) strip of cardboard

One skein each of two colours of crewel wool

Pencil

Embroidery scissors

Small comb

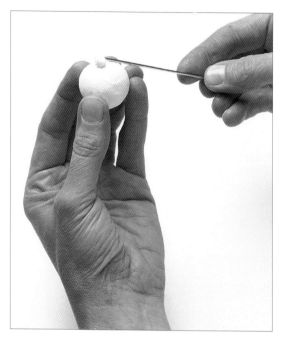

1 Using the crochet hook or meat skewer, start to pull out the centre of the paper ball. At first only small pieces of paper will tear off at a time.

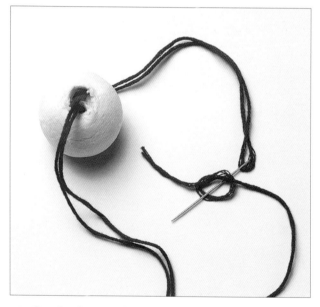

2 The paper will then start to unravel out of the centre like a narrow ribbon. Remove enough paper so that a pencil will slide easily through the centre of the ball. The hole will be larger on one side than the other and this will be made use of later. The paper ball, or body, is now ready to be covered.

3 Cut 2m (78in) of each colour of stranded cotton. Starting with the main colour, make a loose knot at one end and thread the other end through the needle. Take the needle through the body and then through the knot. Pull the knot up the thread and tighten it near the body. Work the knot into the centre of the body to hide it.

4 Thread up the second colour and secure it as for the first. To wrap the threads around the body, pass the needle through the centre as many times as required. Either use the threads to make a pattern or wrap them round randomly. When the body is completely covered, put it aside.

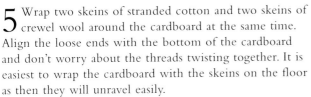

5 Wrap two skeins of stranded cotton and two skeins of crewel wool around the cardboard at the same time. Align the loose ends with the bottom of the cardboard and don't worry about the threads twisting together. It is easiest to wrap the cardboard with the skeins on the floor as then they will unravel easily.

6 To secure the skirt, take a 20cm (8in) piece of embroidery cotton, fold it in half and push the looped end under the wound yarn at the top of the card. Pass the loose ends through the loop and pull it tight. Slide the wound yarn off the cardboard and make a double knot around it with the loose ends of the tie. Put the skirt to one side.

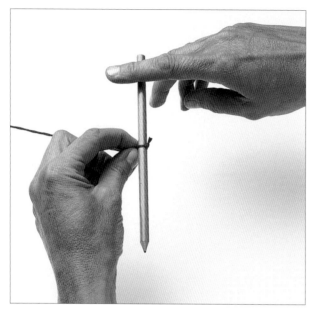

7 Cut four pieces of stranded cotton, each three times longer than the finished length of the loop you require. Tie the pieces together with a knot at each end. Slip one end over a hook or door handle with two strands on each side. Put a pencil between the strands at the other end and turn it round and round to twist the strands together. Stop twisting when the cotton starts to fold back on itself. Remove the cotton from the hook and, holding both knotted ends together, let it twist round on itself to produce a cord eight strands thick.

8 Using one end of the skirt's securing tie, stitch one end of the cord to the skirt. Stitch the other end of the cord to the skirt with the other end of the tie.

TIP: *Tassels will always look skimpy and rather homemade if the skirt is not full enough. This always takes more yarn than you think it will, so don't be surprised if your skirt bundle looks big — it should do.*

Always try to use more than one type of fibre in the skirt, this gives it texture and fullness. Embroidery thread alone will give a rather limp skirt whereas wool alone gives a skirt with no gloss.

9 Fold a scrap of thread in half, pass the loop through the top of the cord and take the loose ends through the loop. Thread the loose ends through a needle and take the needle through the centre of the body, going up through the larger hole and out of the smaller one. Pull the cord through and remove the loop of scrap thread.

10 Push the body down the cord until the top of the skirt disappears inside it. Cut through the loops of thread at the bottom of the tassel.

ABOVE *Once you have mastered the basic tassel, try adding beads and embroidery to the body.*

LEFT *Arabian tassels also make excellent additions to cushions.*

11 To tidy the skirt, give it a thorough combing. Then, holding it firmly in one hand, trim across the ends to even them up.

DISPLAYING A COLLECTION

Any collection is a deeply personal thing and you should display it in a manner which brings out the best in both it and the room it is in. Whatever you display, analyse all the elements carefully to make sure that the collection and its surroundings work harmoniously. The collection must complement the decorative scheme of the room, the furniture it is on or near, and the atmosphere of the room. A collection of jolly china pigs, no matter how sweet, would simply not look good in this room.

Often, in a drawing room, one finds that classic meets contemporary, and the two can work extremely well together. With a mantlepiece of such enormous proportions and beauty as this one, you need something fairly significant and substantial to set it off and break it up. This collection of brass candlesticks is both eclectic and unusual and yet it fits very well into its formal surroundings.

The gleaming golden colour of the candlesticks beautifully complements the salmon-pink coloured walls and the gilt frames of the paintings. Their height breaks up the length of the mantlepiece and at the same time draws attention to the high ceiling, which is such a spectacular feature in older houses. An oval painting set between the square and rectangular ones creates the perfect equilibrium above the white Italian marble fireplace with its rectangular pink granite panels.

Candlelight is so very beautiful – so soft, so romantic, so flattering. However, there are a couple of practical points to bear in mind. The candles should be non-drip to avoid spilling wax on your furniture and, of course, you must never leave lighted candles unattended, no matter how far from anything flammable they are. I like to stick to ivory-coloured candles at all times, but you may find that coloured ones would suit your own room well.

THE Guest BEDOOM

Choosing a colour scheme for a guest bedroom needs careful thought. It must be neither too masculine or too feminine or either way, some of your guests may not feel very comfortable. This fresh cornflower blue and yellow is an excellent solution as it fulfils this criteria well and it looks very inviting.

Quintet-pleated curtains have enormous presence and style due to their large size and fullness. Choosing this heading for your window treatment means that you have to have a lovely pole. The range of poles and finials available today is huge, so you will be spoilt for choice. Remember that the pole is, in effect, replacing the pelmet, so it is worth investing in a wonderful one as it will make a big difference to the look of your window treatment.

The perfectly matched blue contrast pleats in the curtain add a little element of surprise that is such fun. This same blue appears in the piping on the deliciously thick window seat. The tassel tieback is so chic, with all the colours carefully matched to those in the curtain and the window seat fabric. I would put

the lampshade in the same league; it is made of a fabulously rich yellow silk and has great depth in its generous pleats. Making, as opposed to buying, a silk lampshade is deeply satisfying since you can then achieve the perfect colour, shape and size to enhance your pretty bedroom.

Contrast Quintet-pleated Curtains

These are the most sumptuous pleats and require a lot of fullness. They also look
brilliant in a pelmet, especially when it is trimmed in heavy bullion, as you get a marvellous
trumpet shape at the hem. They are a strong enough statement without the
addition of the blue contrast, but this does look fabulous and only requires a little more effort.

MATERIALS

Main fabric

Interlining

Lining

Contrast fabric or ribbon

Fusible buckram

Fan edging

MEASURING

The same as The Classic Curtain
(see page 10)

CUTTING THE FABRICS

Main fabric, interlining and lining:
the same as The Classic Curtain
*(see page 10) but allow three times
fullness across the width and
18cm (7in) turndown at the top for
the heading.*

Contrast fabric – two strips per
pleat: *either 7 x 16cm (2³⁄₄ x
6¹⁄₄in) strips of fabric or 3 x 16cm
(1¹⁄₄ x 6¹⁄₄in) lengths of ribbon.*

Fusible buckram: *15cm (6in) by
the width of the main fabric.*

Make up the curtain as for The
Classic Curtain *(see page 10) to
step 18; there should be 18cm (7in)
of the main fabric above the finished
drop measurement. Lay out the
curtain and work out the
positioning of the pleats. Measure
5cm (2in) in from each edge and
mark with a vertical pin. Measure
25cm (10in), the width needed for
a quintet pleat, from each pin and
again, mark with a vertical pin.
Measure the distance between the
two inner pins. Each pleat is 25cm
(10in), and each gap between the
pleats about 12cm (4³⁄₄in). Work
out how many pleats you can fit
across the finished width. Mark the
pleats with vertical pins at what
will be the top of the curtain, 18cm
(7in) from the raw edge. Now
measure out the individual pleats by
dividing each 25cm (10in) section
by five and marking each point with
a vertical pin.*

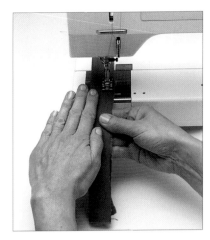

1 Wrong sides facing, fold the strips of contrast fabric in half lengthways and machine down the long edge, a taking 0.5cm (¼in) seam allowance. Turn the seam to the back and press. Tuck 1cm (½in) of the end of the tube inside itself, adjust it until the end is square and press it flat to make a neat end.

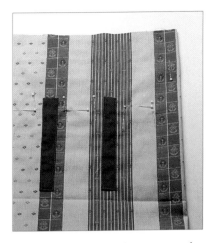

2 Pin a strip over pleats two and four, with the top of the strips 17cm (6¾in) down from the cut edge. Topstitch down both long sides and across the neatened end.

3 Lay the strip of fusible buckram between the lining and interlining, aligning the top edge of the buckram with the raw edges.

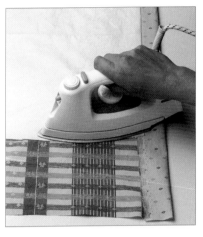

4 Fold the lining over the buckram and iron it to fuse it to the fabrics.

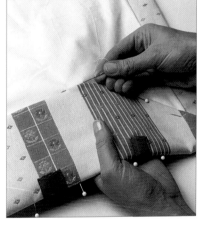

5 Turn the unlined top section of the main fabric over to lie on top of the lining. Turn under a 3cm (1¼in) hem and pin. Turn the corner under to make a right angle and slip stitch down the diagonal and along the hem.

6 Wrong sides facing, fold each 25cm (10in) quintet pleat section in half, matching the pins, and hold it in place with a clamp or a clothespeg.

7 Machine down from the outside pin to the bottom of the buckram in a straight line.

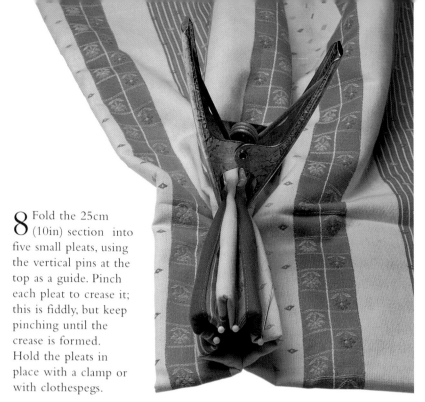

8 Fold the 25cm (10in) section into five small pleats, using the vertical pins at the top as a guide. Pinch each pleat to crease it; this is fiddly, but keep pinching until the crease is formed. Hold the pleats in place with a clamp or with clothespegs.

9 Stitch through the bottom of each pleated section with strong button thread to hold it in place, catching each pleat. Stitch through twice and anchor the thread at the back.

10 Stitch right through the top of each pleated section, catching each pleat. Stitch through once and anchor the thread at the back.

11 Pin the fan edge to the back of the leading edge of the curtain, with the top of the webbing aligned with the edge of the curtain so that just the fan shows at the front. Hand stitch it in place through the webbing.

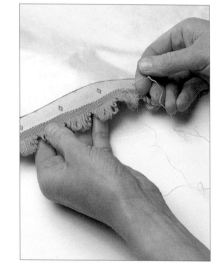

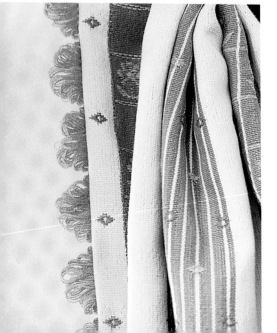

12 Push a pin hook into the back of the curtain, about halfway up the pleat. Make sure that the pin goes into the fabric, not into the line of machining, as it will break the stitches.

PATTERNS IN A COLOURWAY

Using different patterns in the same colourway is the obvious answer to a co-ordinated look, and it is enormous fun. But it is important that you don't overdo it or the eye will be confused.

You can create a successful look by using three or four patterns in a colourway for the curtains, window seat and perhaps the dressing table, and then introducing something totally different for the bed valance, the bedcover, the cushions and the chair covers. If the fabric patterns in the room are, so far, rather busy, go for solid, single colours. Remember that the harmony in the room is of the utmost importance. It is the introduction of this single colour that can pull the whole room together.

1 *Collette J4227.*

2 *Martine J4252.*

3 *Francesca J4232.*

4 *Jeanne J4242.*

5 *Juliette J4237.*

6 *Helene J4237.*

Piped Window Seat Cover

A window seat is a charming feature in any room. To put a cushion on it is even better, especially a thick, feather-filled cushion covered in a fabric that tones with other furnishings in the room. This is an easy project, as long as you have a good piping foot on your machine, and the result is stunning.

MATERIALS

Main fabric
Contrast fabric
Piping cord
Window seat cushion

MEASURING

The length, width and depth of the cushion.

CUTTING THE MATERIALS

If you are using a patterned fabric, the top and bottom of the cushion should be pattern matched to the band.

Main fabric – top and bottom

Length: *the length of the cushion plus 3cm (1¼in).*

Width: *the width of the cushion plus 3cm (1¼in).*

Main fabric – band front and back

Length: *the length of the cushion plus 3cm (1¼in).*

Depth: *the depth of the cushion plus 3cm (1¼in).*

Main fabric – band sides

Length: *the width of the cushion plus 3cm (1¼in).*

Depth: *the depth of the cushion plus 3cm (1¼in).*

If you have enough fabric and can make the pattern match, this band could be cut as one strip.

Contrast piping fabric: *40cm (16in) square.*

Piping cord: *twice the circumference of the cushion.*

1 Make up piping in the contrast fabric as shown in steps 7–11 of *Gathered Valance* (see page 36). Right side up, pin the piping to the edge of the top of the cover. Align the raw edges and clip the corners to help the piping lie flat. Machine it in place with a zipper or piping foot, stitching close to the cord.

2 To join the ends of the piping, cut the cord so that the two ends butt up together. Trim the fabric on one end level with the cord, and on the other end 2cm (¾in) longer than the cord. Turn under 1cm (½in) of the long end of fabric and lay this over the raw edge of the short end. Pin in place and machine as normal.

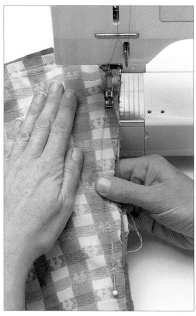

3 Right sides facing, machine the band pieces together to make a strip, leaving a side and back edge unjoined. Machine the band to the piped top, just inside the line of machining that attaches the piping to the cover. Machine all round, matching the pattern carefully.

Tassel Tieback

These tiebacks are seriously expensive to buy, so the obvious answer is to make them. They are a beautiful luxury item in a window treatment and have enormous class. Being able to pick exactly the colours you need to match your fabric is a joy. These tiebacks look so hugely complicated, but you will see from our simple steps that anyone can make one.

MATERIALS

Wooden tassel mould

Cling film

Thin wooden dowel (or rod)

Spray glue

Gimp (or strong, very thin furnishing cord)

Strong sewing thread in a neutral colour

Decorative cord

Heavy wire, approx 10cm (4in) longer than the tassel mould.

Pliers

Piece of strong card 2cm (3/4in) deeper than finished length of the tassel skirt and one-and-a-half times longer than the circumference of the waist of the tassel mould.

For a three-colour tassel: two skeins of crewel wool, four skeins of stranded embroidery thread and one reel of sewing thread in each colour.

Masking tape

Knitting needle

Fine wire, approx 20cm (8in) longer than the circumference of the waist of the tassel mould.

MEASURING

One piece of cord 30cm (12in) long. One piece measured as for Plaited Tieback with Rosette (see page 20).

The skirt of the tassel should be approximately twice as long as the measurement of the tassel mould from top to waist.

4 Pipe the bottom section of the cover the same way as the top. Machine the band to the bottom as in step 3. Leave a 40cm (16in) gap along the back of the cover un-stitched. Push the cushion through the gap and slip stitch it closed.

1 Wrap cling film around the bottom of the tassel mould and around the top of the dowel. Push the dowel into the hole in the base of the mould. Spray the top section of the mould with glue and wait until it does not 'lift' when you touch it. Wrap the gimp around the mould, starting from the top, with each coil butting tightly up to the next one so that the mould is completely covered. Remove the cling film and the dowel.

2 Cut 2m (78in) of strong thread and double it. Lay the looped end around the waist of the mould and thread the cut ends through the loop. Knot the cut ends 10cm (4in) from the end. Wind all the thread around the waist until you reach the knot. Split the two cut ends and wind them round the waist in opposite directions then knot them together.

3 Either make a cord following step 7 of the *Arabian Tassel* (see page 86) or buy a length. If you make one, use some crewel wool and some embroidery thread to make a thick cord. The cord should be approximately 20cm (5in) long. Stitch the ends of the cord together. Make a small loop in one end of the heavy wire and stitch the ends of the cord firmly to it.

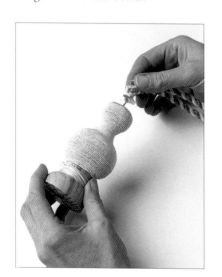

4 Thread the wire through the tassel mould from top to bottom.

5 Pull the wire through the tassel mould until the ends of the cord and the wire loop sit snugly in the hole at the top. Bend the loose end of the wire into a coil that is too big to pull back up through the hole.

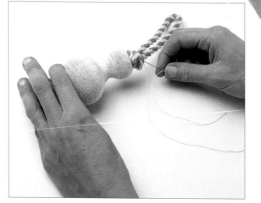

6 Tie a loose knot in the loop of cord and push it down until it sits on top of the tassel mould. Pull it tight, pushing it down at the same time. Stitch through it a few times to ensure it will not come loose.

7 Cut a notch in each side of the card approximately 2cm (¾in) from the top. Cut another small notch in the top and bottom approximately 3cm (1¼in) from the left-hand side. Cut a 3m (117in) length of strong thread and double it. Lay it around the card, slotting it into the top and bottom notches, with the loop in front, at the top. Thread the cut ends through the loop and pull it tight, then separate the ends and slot one into each side notch to hold them out of the way.

8 Keeping aside one skein of wool for the ruff, unravel the skeins and reels of wool and threads, lay them all together and from now on treat them as one item: the skirt materials. Always use a mix of types of thread and wool in a tassel skirt as it makes for a more interesting, textured look. Tape the end of the skirt materials to the bottom of the back of the card, in line with the loop of strong thread. Take them to the front, then up to and over the top.

9 Unhitch the lengths of strong thread from the side notches and tie them over the strand of skirt materials using a 4-twist knot. This is exactly like a single knot but one thread is looped around the other four times instead of the usual once. Continue in this way, winding and tying the yarn, until you have made a skirt 1cm (½in) longer than the circumference of the waist of the tassel mould. Tie the threads in a firm reef knot but do not cut them.

TIP: *There is such a wide range of threads available these days that it should be possible to match any colour scheme. Remember to take fabric swatches with you when buying threads so that you get the best match. Don't rely on your memory as often colour variations are very subtle.*

10 Cut through the skirt materials along the bottom of the card. Cut the loop of strong thread you started with.

11 Tie the ends of the strong thread from one side of the skirt (the knotted end or the cut loop), to the thread that is wrapped around the waist of the tassel mould. Use a 4-twist knot.

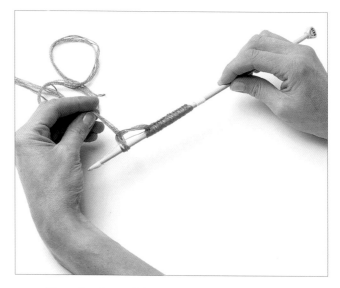

12 Wrap the skirt around the waist of the tassel mould and tie the strong threads at the other end to the waist threads.

13 To make the ruff, lay the fine wire along the knitting needle and tape it in place, leaving 5cm (2in) free at each end. Unravel the skein of wool and fold it into one length, three strands thick. Double this, lay it over the needle close to the tape at one end of the wire, thread the cut ends through the loop and pull it tight. Working with all six strands, make the ruff by winding the wool round the needle and threading it under itself, then pulling the newly formed loop tightly up to the last loop.

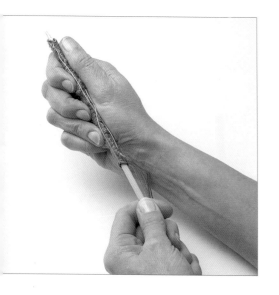

14 When the ruff is as long as the circumference of the tassel waist, un-tape the ends of the wire and fold them over the ruff to keep it in place. Slide the ruff off the needle. Make two ruffs in this way.

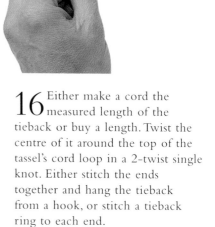

15 Tie a ruff around the waist of the tassel mould by twisting the ends of the wire together. Twist loosely at first, adjust the ruff so that the 'seam' is underneath and then twist the wire up tightly. Cut the ends of the wire short and bend them over underneath the ruff. The ends of the ruff wool simply join the tassel skirt. Add the second ruff below the first. Comb the skirt and trim it as in step 11 of the *Arabian Tassel* (see page 86).

16 Either make a cord the measured length of the tieback or buy a length. Twist the centre of it around the top of the tassel's cord loop in a 2-twist single knot. Either stitch the ends together and hang the tieback from a hook, or stitch a tieback ring to each end.

Pleated Silk Lampshade

This is not a quick project and you must have very clean hands at all times when you are making it. However, having exactly the right-coloured lampshade to best enhance your room is such a wonderful luxury that making one yourself completely worth the effort. All you need to do is follow the steps, fitting and pinning with great care.

MATERIALS

Lampshade frame
White cotton tape
White or ivory silk lining fabric
Main silk fabric
Strong upholstery thread

MEASURING

The lampshade frame.

CUTTING THE MATERIALS

Tape: *three times the circumference of the top and base of the frame plus three times the length of the two side struts.*

Lining fabric width: *two diamond shapes (cut on the cross), each half the circumference of the base of the frame plus 10cm (4in) at their widest point.*

Lining fabric length: *From the middle to the top point, the height of the frame plus approx 15cm (6in). (Before it comes to a point, the top of the diamond must be wider that half the circumference of the top of the lampshade.)*

Main fabric length: *The height of the frame plus 5cm (2in).*

Main fabric width: *three times the circumference of the base of the frame. Divide this measurement by the width of the silk fabric to give you the number of fabric widths you will need. Do not join the widths.*

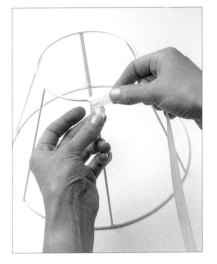

1 To start taping, wrap the tape around the top of a strut (one where the fitting for the light bulb joins the frame) and back over itself, catching the end in.

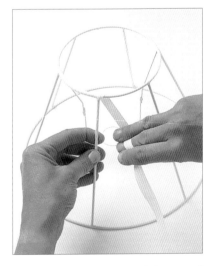

2 Wrap the tape around the top of the frame smoothly and tightly, overlapping half the width of the tape on each wrap. Do not wrap the tape in a figure eight around the top of the struts as this is too bulky: simply wrap over them.

3 Tape the top and base of the frame, and the two side struts where the fitting for the light bulb joins the frame. Always start taping in the same way and secure the other end of the tape with a stitch.

4 With the top point of the diamond positioned centrally above and between the taped side struts, pin the lining fabric to the top of the frame at the sides.

5 Pull the fabric taut and pin it in the following order: at the top and bottom corners, in the centre of the side struts, down the side struts, at the top where each strut joins the ring and at the bottom where each strut joins the ring.

TIP: *You can make a lampshade from any fairly fine fabric, though silk undoubtedly works best. Don't use a patterned fabric as the tight pleating will mean that the effect of the pattern is completely lost and your lampshade can end up looking a bit of a mess.*

Before you make a shade, hold your chosen fabric up to the light and make sure that you like the effect of the light shining through it. Very strongly coloured fabrics can produce an odd glow so be careful. Lining should always be white or ivory, as a colour can alter the colour of the main fabric.

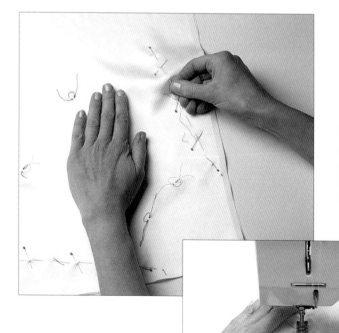

6 Remove the pins from the frame but slip them back into the lining in exactly the same places. Lay this piece of lining over the other and tack the two pieces of lining together down the line of pins at each side. Make a tailor's tack at each pin marking where the struts joined the top and bottom of the frame.

7 Take the pins out and machine 0.5cm (¼in) outside the line of tacking. Zigzag just outside the line of machining, or make a second line of straight machining.

8 Cut out the lining, cutting close to the zigzagging at the sides but leaving 4cm (1½in) above and below the lines of tailor's tacks. Set the lining aside.

9 Turn under 2cm (¾in) on the short edge of one strip of the main fabric. Pin the turned-under edge to the bottom of the frame, 1cm (½in) from the raw edge of the fabric. Pull the fabric taut and pin the edge to the top. Make sure that this turned-under edge runs in a straight line from top to bottom of the frame. Turn the frame upside down and start to pleat the fabric along the base of the frame. Fold the fabric every 5cm (2in) and pin it 1cm (½in) from the last pleat. Pin three pleats then stitch them in place with strong upholstery thread. Oversew through the pleats into the tape on the frame, stitching right on the bottom of the base of the frame. Leave the first two pleats only pinned.

10 Once you have completed a width, pinning and stitching three pleats at a time, turn the frame right side up. Pull the fabric taut then pleat and stitch the top in the same way. Condense the pleats a little to keep them running straight (they should be parallel to the struts). Oversew the pleats to the tape, right on top of the frame. Hold the shade over a lit light bulb and check that the pleats look even with light shining through them.

11 To join a new width, turn under 2cm (¾in) along a short edge and pin the width to the frame, top and bottom, overlapping the raw edge of the last width and keeping the spacing between the pleats even. Pin and stitch the pleats to the bottom and top of the frame, joining in new widths as necessary, until you have covered the whole frame.

12 To join the end of the last strip to the beginning of the first strip, unpin the first two pleats. Trim any excess fabric from the last strip and tuck the raw end under the turned-under end of the first strip. Arrange the pleats so that they are even and stitch them in place. Do a final check over a lit light bulb to make sure that all the pleats look even.

13 Trim away excess fabric close to the stitching at the top and bottom of the lampshade.

14 Wrong sides facing, slip the lining into the frame. Snip the stitches on the lining seams enough to allow the fabric to fit around the side struts as shown. Pin in place.

15 Pin the tailor's tacks to the top of the struts, snipping the lining as you go to fit it in place.

16 Turn the lampshade upside down. Pull the lining fabric taut and pin it to the base of the frame, starting at the side seams. Stitch the lining to the frame, oversewing at the front of the frame to avoid the stitches holding the main fabric to the frame.

17 On the cross, cut two strips of lining material 3.5cm (1⅜in) wide by 12cm (4¾in) long. Fold each into three widthways and press lightly. With the raw edges underneath, wrap a strip under each side strut and cross them on top. Pin and stitch in place. These 'bandages' cover the raw edges around the struts. Trim the ends close to the stitching.

18 On the cross, cut a strip of the main fabric 5cm (2in) wide and long enough to fit around the bottom of the lampshade; join strips if necessary. Fit a strip to the bottom of the frame, pulling it very tight.

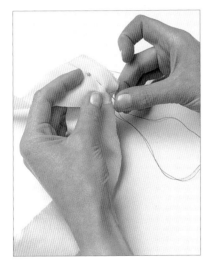

19 Tack the ends of the strip together. Fit it to the bottom of the frame again to ensure that it is tight. Machine the ends together to make a circle. Cut and fit a strip for the top of the lampshade in exactly the same way.

20 Wrong sides facing, fold the circles in half. With the raw side at the front of the frame, oversew the strips to the top and bottom of the frame, making sure that the stitches sit right on top of the frame.

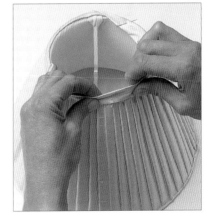

21 Pull the folded edge of the circle down over the stitches and the raw edges. Trim the raw edges if necessary. If needed, a dab of clear-drying glue can be used to hold the turn-down in place.

A GUEST'S **DRESSING** TABLE

When your guest arrives, after what is likely to have been a long journey, you want everything to absolutely perfect for them. The bedside lights should already be on (if it is late in the day), as this looks particularly welcoming. Ideally your guest should never have to ask you for anything; it often makes people feel awkward. Everything they need should be in the room waiting for them. Of course, sometimes people ask for odd things, but try and predict as far as possible what they will need.

The dressing table is usually a focal point in the room, and as such you should try to make it look especially pretty. On the dressing table there should be a very special variety of everything your guest may need. If, as is often the case, the room does not have a private bathroom, you should put all toiletries on the dressing table, or they will become confused with those already in the bathroom.

The soap must be large and delicious and there must be a more than usual abundance of delicious 'smellies': bath oil, shower gels, scented talcum powder and shampoo. You also need to put out tissues, cleansing pads and china toothmugs. There must be adequate space on the dressing table for all of this and your guest's sponge bag and some personal belongings.

A clock not only looks good but is dead handy for those who forget theirs. Flowers are totally essential as they offer special touch of love and welcome for your guests. Pot pourri smells delicious and is an added bonus in case your flower arrangement has no scent.

Writing paper is absolutely essential, you never know when you are going to need it, even if is just for writing a vital little note on. Also provide a pen, as the paper will be useless without it.

Fresh water in a decanter is always welcome and you can make an attractive display of it with pretty glasses on a tray covered with a crisp linen cloth.

THE Conservatory DINING ROOM

Whe entertaining, even when it is just the family, a pretty table setting, however simple, always creates a lovely atmosphere. The breakfast, lunch, tea or dinner is immediately elevated into something special as opposed to something mundane. Quilted tablemats, together with a table runner, are extremely practical as they keep the table, or tablecloth clean for many days.

As conservatories have such large expanses of glass the window treatment should always be as warm-looking as possible, since when you entertain at night, you want maximum psychological and physical warmth. Roman blinds are the perfect answer since they cause almost no light loss when pulled up yet, when let down, they create a cosy, warm atmosphere that is perfect for evening dining.

This fabric is so textured and inviting that it almost resembles thin carpet. But, as a total contrast to this, the slightly shiny, grosgrain ribbon brings extraordinary life to this woolly fabric. The waffle-like buttons are a further piece of collage in low-relief.

All the different greens on the table, set against their fabric backdrop, blend beautifully together to make a thoroughly stylish room.

Buttoned Roman Blind

This is a most practical and attractive way to curtain a conservatory successfully as there is so little light loss when the blinds are pulled up. Roman blinds use extremely little fabric compared to curtains so you can go to town and choose something really special, as we have here. You need a large table and clamps to make the project easily, and all the measuring must be very precise.

MATERIALS

Main fabric

Grosgrain ribbon

Lining fabric

1cm (¹⁄₂in) diameter dowling rods

Plastic rings

Thin wooden batten

1.5cm (⁵⁄₈in) covered buttons (see Suppliers, page 126).

MEASURING

Exactly the required finished length and width (see page 123).

CUTTING THE FABRICS

Main fabric width: *the finished width plus 5cm (2in) on each side. If pattern matching, remember that the full width must be in the middle. Perfect symmetry is vital.*

Main fabric length: *the finished length plus 5cm (2in) top and bottom.*

Ribbon: *the length of both long sides and one short side of the finished blind, plus 10cm (4in).*

Lining fabric width: *the finished width of the blind.*

Lining fabric length: *the finished length of the blind plus 5cm (2in) for every rod (see below), plus 3cm (1¹⁄₄in) at the top.*

Dowling rods: *6cm (2¹⁄₂in) shorter than the finished width of the blind.*

Wooden batten: *0.5 x 5cm (¹⁄₄ x 2in) by the finished width of the blind minus 4cm (1¹⁄₂in).*

POSITIONING THE RODS

Rod cases are usually between 18cm (7in) and 22cm (8³⁄₄in) apart. The ideal set of measurements for a blind is as follows:

25cm (10in) from top of the blind to the highest rod.

20cm (8in) between each rod.

10cm (4in) between the lowest rod and the hem.

You can vary these measurements a little, but try not to reduce the distances at the top and bottom.

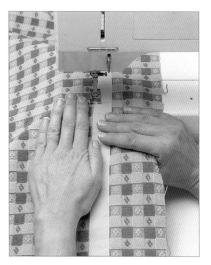

1 The ribbon border runs down both long sides and across the bottom, but not across the top. Machine the ribbon, stitching very close to the edge, to the main fabric, 8cm (3in) from the edge.

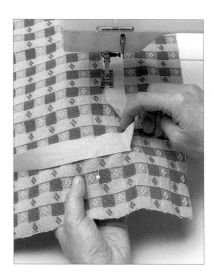

2 At the corners, fold the ribbon as shown to make a mitre. Machine both sides of the ribbon and hand-sew the mitres.

3 Turn the fabric over and press 5cm (2in) to the back on all sides. Press in a 6cm (2½in) triangle at the corners. Fold the sides in to make a mitre and hand-sew it together (see inset).

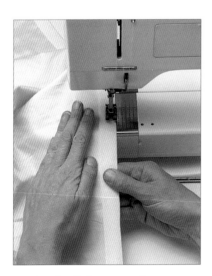

4 On the lining, press 3cm (1¼in) to the back and make mitres as for the main fabric. Machine the soft side of the Velcro to the lining, leaving a 3cm (1¼in) 'tail' of Velcro either side. To make the later slip stitching easier, position the Velcro 3mm (⅛in) below the top edge of the lining.

5 Measure the distance from the top of the blind to the first rod, add 2.5cm (1in), and press a fold across the lining at this point.

6 Measure down 2.5cm (1in) from the fold and make a scratch on the fabric with a pin. Mark several points in this way, then use a ruler to join all the scratches with one long scratch. Machine across the scratch to make a rod case, reversing at each end to finish. Repeat steps 5 and 6, measuring down to the next rod each time, until you have made all the rod cases needed.

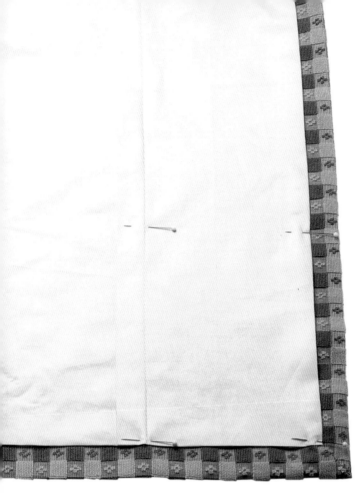

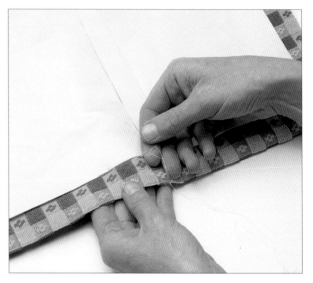

7 Lay the lining on the back of the main fabric. The Velcro at the top should align with the folded top of the main fabric and there should be a 3cm (1¼in) border round the other three sides. Pin lining in place.

8 Slip stitch the lining to the main fabric down both sides, as far as the lowest rod case. Make sure that you leave the channels free and the bottom hem open.

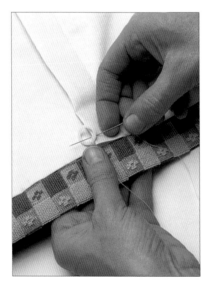

9 On the lines of machining, spot stitch the lining to the main fabric every 30cm (12in) across the blind. Stab stitch (see page 125) from the back to the front twice and tie threads firmly at the back.

10 Sew plastic rings to the rod cases at the edge and in the middle of the blind.

11 Feed the dowels into the rod cases. Oversew the ends of each case closed.

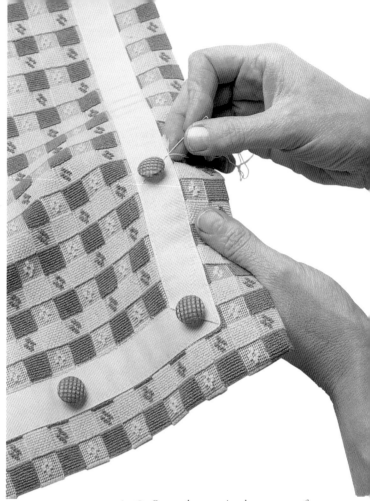

12 Slip the wooden batten into the hem of the blind. Slip stitch the lining to the main fabric down the unsewn parts of the sides and across the hem.

13 Sew a button in the centre of the ribbon every 8cm (3in).

TIP: *Adding a border to a Roman blind turns what can be a rather plain window treatment into an interesting one, and it is easy to do. You can make a border from almost any flat braid or ribbon.*

For an extra-special touch, cut strips of fabric used for another soft furnishing project in the room and use these as a border. Cut the fabric strips to fit your blind then turn under a narrow edge on each long and short side of the strip. Position the strips on the blind, butting up the edges, and topstitch them in place.

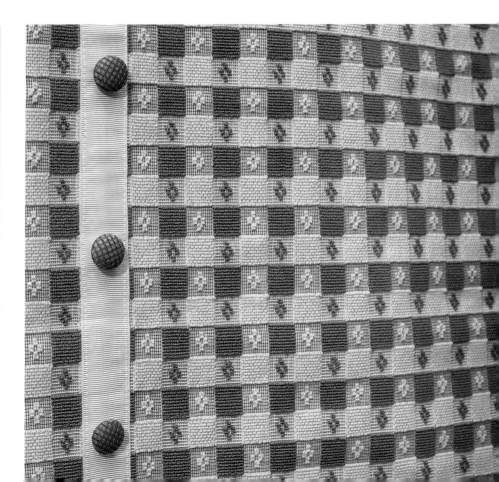

Quilted Table Mat

These are wonderfully quick and easy to make and a set would make a
marvellous present for a friend. They do not have to be quilted, though this detail
looks beautiful and helps to protect your table from the heat of the plates.
As well as making a table setting look very special, they are practical and wash easily.

MATERIALS

Main fabric

50g (2oz) wadding

Backing fabric

MEASURING

The size of the finished tablemat

CUTTING THE MATERIALS

Main fabric: *the finished size.*

Wadding: *the finished size plus
1cm (¹⁄₂in) all round.*

Backing fabric: *the finished size
plus 3.5cm (1³⁄₈in) all round.*

1 Lay the wadding
in the centre of
the backing fabric,
then lay the main
fabric in the centre
of the wadding.

2 Pin all the layers together, with
the rows of pins running
diagonally across the mat. Use a lot
of pins as it is important that the
layers do not slip during the
quilting. We followed the pattern of
the fabric and quilted the mat into
squares. Start machine quilting
from the centre and work across to
one edge. Turn the mat round and
quilt the other half. Then turn the
mat 90° and quilt lines in the other
direction, again working from the
middle to the edges.

3 Trim away any excess wadding all round the mat.

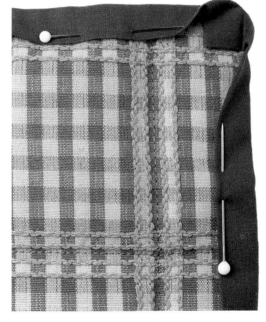

4 At the corners, fold the point of the backing fabric over the main fabric, as shown. Along the sides, fold the backing fabric in half, so that the raw edge lies against the raw edge of the main fabric. Turn the backing fabric over again, so that it encloses the raw edges of the main fabric, and pin. At the corners, the folded sides will make a mitre.

TIP: *These tablemats are a brilliant project for using up pieces of fabric left over from other projects. In this way you not only get new mats, but they co-ordinate with your room as well. Choose a plain backing fabric as it is very difficult to make the quilting follow a pattern on the front and back of the mat.*

5 Topstitch the backing fabric close to the folded edge all round the mat. As the mitred corners are small, they should be held in place by the line of machining. However, if necessary, hand-stitch each of the mitres closed.

Fringed Table Runner

A runner looks so pretty and adds so much to the inviting look of a laid table.
It is fun to contrast it with the table mats, or you can make it from the same fabric.
They are the work of minutes to produce and so you can make them for special occasions:
they look wonderful in Christmas fabrics for example.

MATERIALS

Fabric

Bullion fringing

MEASURING

Length: *the length of the table.*

Width: *one-third of the width of the table.*

CUTTING THE MATERIALS

Fabric length: *the length of the table plus 60cm (24in).*

Fabric width: *twice the measured width plus 2cm (¾in).*

Bullion fringing: *twice the measured width plus 8cm (3in).*

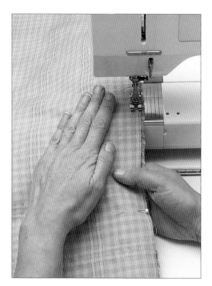

1 Right sides facing, fold the fabric in half widthways. Machine the raw edges together and press the seam open. Turn the tube right side out, turn the seam to centre back and press the runner.

2 Turn under and press 1cm (½in) at each short end. Topstitch these ends shut.

3 Cut the piece of bullion in half. Fold over 2cm (¾in) at each end and top stitch it across one end of the right side of the runner. Repeat at the other end.

PATTERNED AND PLAIN TEXTURES

Textured fabrics give a new element to your soft furnishings. Their three-dimensional character and flocked or embroidered surfaces adds luxury and therefore an impression of warmth and comfort.

Fabrics like this are brilliant in a conservatory, which as an outdoor garden room, starts out at a disadvantage in terms of warmth, from both the physical and psychological point of view, if you want to use it as a dining room.

Shades of yellows are some of the warmest colours ever, especially when they are of an egg-yolk hue. Mixing these with texture results in a perfect atmosphere for a room where warm carpets, upholstered furniture and thick curtains are lacking.

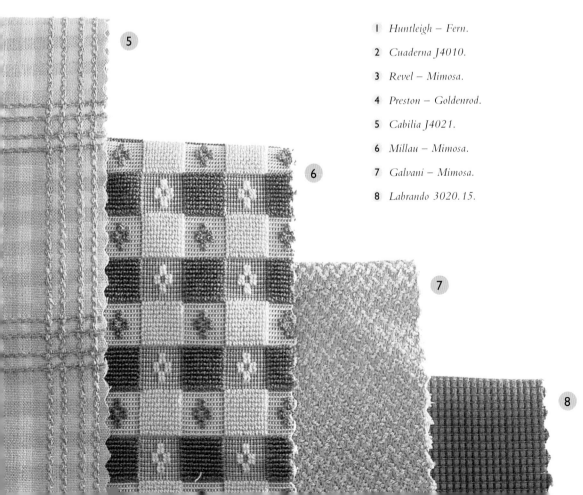

1 *Huntleigh – Fern.*

2 *Cuaderna J4010.*

3 *Revel – Mimosa.*

4 *Preston – Goldenrod.*

5 *Cabilia J4021.*

6 *Millau – Mimosa.*

7 *Galvani – Mimosa.*

8 *Labrando 3020.15.*

SETTING A TABLE

The way you set a table is so important in terms of the effect and atmosphere you want to create. A pretty table setting makes your guest feel really welcome and that their hostess has thoroughly enjoyed the thought and preparation involved in the production of the breakfast, lunch, tea or dinner. Equally, the setting should suggest that your guest can expect some wonderful food. Napkins, table mats, table runners, tablecloths, cutlery, china, glass, candlesticks and flowers should all combine to offer some kind of celebration – however low-key.

If your starter is cold, it looks extremely pretty if it is already at each place when you sit down at the table. From a practical point of view, this means you can all sit down together and not have the disruption of the hostess having to fetch the food, having already seated everyone. Always light the candles before your guests arrive at the table, unlit candles make a table look dead and cold. Pour out water into the tumblers in advance. Salt and pepper should be easily accessible for everyone, so make sure there are plenty of sets of them. The same goes for butter, sauces, bread, biscuits and chocolates. Wine should also be opened in advance and set on the table. Cheese should always be unwrapped.

Fabric table mats, as well as looking extremely pretty, are ideal for keeping a tablecloth or surface clean. It is so easy to pick them up at the end of the evening and shake them, and they launder easily. Table runners are fun and pull the whole table setting together. You might choose 'everyday' china and cutlery for a more informal or family occasion, while saving your best stuff for more special occasions.

Finally, make sure your guests are not too cold or too hot. I have memories of a house in Scotland where you just had to hug your hot dinner plate because you were so cold. Equally, when you were given a baked potato, you derived more pleasure from holding it than from eating it.

Tools and Equipment

The basic tools and materials that you need for the projects in this book are few and easy to get hold of. In addition, a trestle table is extremely useful for curtain making if you have the space. This is much longer than the usual kitchen table and so makes it easier to cope with the lengths of fabric.

In the materials lists for each project, the basic items such as scissors, needle and matching threads are not listed, as they will always be needed. Also, you should always make up the projects taking a 1.5cm (⅝in) seam allowance, unless otherwise stated.

Deep pencil pleat tape
15cm (6in) wide. Use this for deep headings and also deeper smocking when the pelmet drop is longer.

Pencil pleat tape Ordinary 8cm-(3in-) wide tape. Use this for the headings of all curtains that you intend to cover with a pelmet. Also use it for smocking, (see *Smocked Pelmet*, page 42)

Clamps Metal clamps are invaluable in curtain making; you need four.

Scissors Small scissors are useful for trimming threads and you need the big pair for cutting out fabrics. Ensure that your fabric scissors are kept purely for cutting fabric and don't become general-purpose scissors.

Pin hooks Use when hanging quintet-pleated curtains (see page 95).

Brass curtain hooks Use these with pencil-pleat tape.

Lead weights To sew in every curtain corner.

Wooden folding ruler 2 m (6 ft)
A ruler like this is an absolute must for measuring window widths and heights.

Coloured thread Select the correct colour to match your fabric.

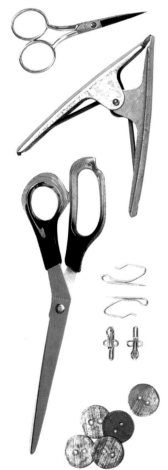

Calculator You must have this for working out fabric quantities, pattern repeats and hand-made pleat sizes.

Staple gun and staples Essential for headboards (see page 28) and noticeboards (see page 56).

Long sharp needles These are known as 'long darners' and you can make good long stitches with them.

Extra long glass-headed pins Once you have used these you will never go back to short ones again.

Fusible buckram You will need this for making quintet pleats (see page 95) and a stiffened band in a pelmet (see page 16).

Small metal ruler This is brilliant for constant measuring while actually sewing. It is also incredibly useful for scraping a fold to produce a sharp line.

Piping cord (size no. 6) For all piping.

Lining and interlining
Lining The best lining fabric is a pure cotton sateen which comes in two widths: 120 cm (48 in) and 137 cm (54 in). It is better to use the wider measure as you will be joining fewer widths. Coloured linings are available, but the colours can fade quickly, especially if your window faces south or west. The neutral colours are ivory (my favourite as the dirt shows less quickly), white, ecru and beige. If ivory isn't available, go for ecru; beige can be terribly dark.
Interlining You can buy interlining, also known as bump, in various weights, but I choose to use medium weight for all my curtains. Anything denser, and the curtains start to become rather heavy.

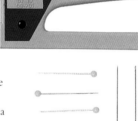

Measuring Windows

Taking careful measurements for curtains, pelmets or blinds is always time well spent.
Write everything down and be prepared to measure everything twice as a double-check. Each
project in this book has detailed instructions, but read these pages for further information.

Measuring Windows for Curtains

HEIGHT

These instructions are for measuring the height of full length
curtains, which, unless there is a good reason for not having
them, such as having an obstruction like a radiator in the way,
are always preferable. If you are making shorter length
curtains, measure from just below the window sill to the
bottom of the pole or pelmet board.

1 Hold the 2m (6ft) folding ruler vertically up the side of the
window with the 2m (6ft) end on the floor. Make a small,
pencil mark on the window frame where the top of the ruler
comes to.

2 Feed the ruler up until you reach the top of the
architrave. If this is very high up, you will have to ask a
friend to stand away from the window to tell you when the
ruler is level with the top of the architrave. This is where you
will place the bottom of the pelmet board, assuming that you
like the height of the window as it is. Note down the two
measurements and add them together.

WIDTH

The chart below will guide you in the calculations of the size
of the housing space (the space needed at either side of the
window for the curtains to stack back into) for different
windows. Allow 10 per cent of the width of your window as
the housing space for the curtains at either side of your
window and you will always be fine.

CURTAIN WIDTHS AND HOUSING SPACE REQUIRED FOR A WINDOW

The number of curtain widths given here is approximate
and is based on material that is 137cm (54in) wide, and
curtains that have medium-weight interlining.

Window width (from edge of architrave to edge of architrave)	housing space (each side of window)	no. of widths in each curtain
50cm (1ft 8in)	5cm (2in)	½
80cm (2ft in)	8cm (3in)	1
1.25m (4ft in)	10cm (4in)	1½
1.6m (5ft 3in)	15cm (6in)	2
1.9m (6ft 3in)	15cm (6in)	2
2.4m (7ft 11in)	20 cm (8in)	2½
2.8m (9ft 2½in)	25cm (1 in)	3
3.3m (10ft 10in)	30cm (12in)	3½
3.8m (12ft 6in)	30cm (12in)	4

Measuring Windows for Pelmets

DROP

1 Tie a handkerchief at the point on your wooden ruler where
you think the finished drop of your pelmet ought to be.

2 Ask a friend to hold up the ruler, level with the top of
your pelmet board. You can now see where the finished
drop of the pelmet will be and if it looks right. One-sixth of
the overall drop of the total window treatment is a good guide.

WIDTH

1 Measure the window width, from architrave to architrave
and add the housing space, as shown in the chart opposite.

2 Then add the pelmet board returns. This is now the
finished width that your pelmet must be.

Measuring Windows for Blinds

There are two positions for a Roman blind. If it is recessed,
take your measurements near to the glass. For the height,
measure from the top of where the mounting batten will be
positioned, to the sill. For the width, measure across the recess.

If the window is not recessed, you are more likely to hang
your blind over the frame. If possible, attach the mounting
batten to the frame itself, but if it isn't flat, screw it to the wall
just above the frame and take your measurements accordingly.

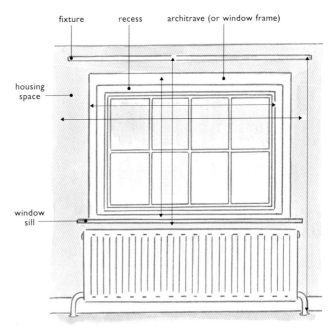

Measuring and Cutting Material

Before measuring, cutting or joining any material, it is essential to check that the grain of the material is straight along the starting edge. To do this, it is easiest to use the square angles of your cutting table, as explained below. Once the material is straight and even, you can start measuring out, cutting and joining widths. At every stage, make use of table clamps which will hold the material in place and make these jobs infinitely easier.

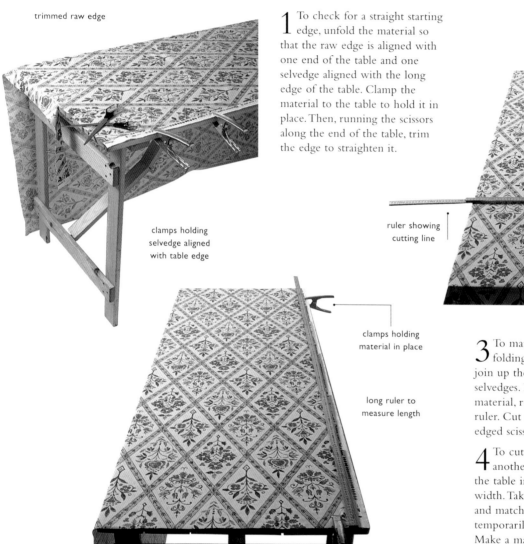

trimmed raw edge

clamps holding
selvedge aligned
with table edge

clamps holding
material in place

long ruler to
measure length

ruler showing
cutting line

1 To check for a straight starting edge, unfold the material so that the raw edge is aligned with one end of the table and one selvedge aligned with the long edge of the table. Clamp the material to the table to hold it in place. Then, running the scissors along the end of the table, trim the edge to straighten it.

3 To mark the cutting line, place the folding ruler across the table and join up the two final marks on the selvedges. Draw a line across the material, running the pen along the ruler. Cut along the line using straight-edged scissors.

4 To cut the remaining widths, unroll another quantity and clamp it to the table in the same way as the first width. Take the first width, already cut, and match its pattern by lining it up temporarily with the uncut material. Make a mark on the selvedge to indicate where the next length of fabric will begin. Measure the distance from the mark just made to the top of the material, so that you can now mark the opposite selvedge the same distance from the top. This removes any excess of pattern repeat, so that the pattern will match at the seams. You are now ready to cut the second width. Repeat the process used for cutting the first width.

2 First, check your calculations and measurements to make sure that they are correct, and that you have enough fabric. With the starting edge still level with one end of the table, unroll the material the whole length of the table and clamp it in place, keeping one selvedge aligned with the long edge. Using the 2m (6ft) folding ruler, measure down along the selvedge as far as the table will allow and mark the selvedge. Then unclamp and unroll more material, moving it onto the table. Again, measure along the selvedge until the total cutting length is reached, and mark the selvedge.

Unclamp, move back to the beginning of the material and measure down the other selvedge in the same way.

Stitches

Use a long sharp needle at all times and always make a strong knot at the end
of your thread before you start sewing. Always finish off your thread securely when you finish
a row of stitching by making several small over-stitches.

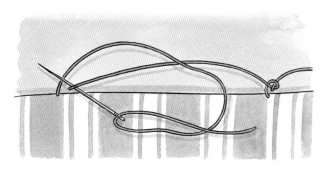

Interlocking

1 Start the row of interlocking stitches by passing the needle through a few grains of the fabric and then stab through the interlining and come up again, having made one running stitch.

2 To make the next stitch, repeat the same process 13cm (5in) further along the fabric. But there is one difference: after you come up from the interlining, take your needle under the thread that is already in place from the previous stitch.

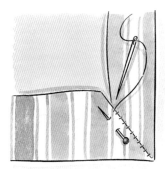

Slip Stitch

1 Come from under the fold with your needle, leaving the knot under the fold and hidden. Come out right at the edge of the fold.

2 Now go back into the other fabric (which is under the fold) at exactly the place where you have just come out. Having gone back in here, now run your needle along as far as it will go, within the fold of the under fabric, and come out on the upper fold again. This leads to an invisible stitch.

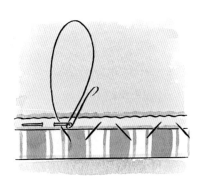

Pyramid Stitch

1 Come up from behind the top fabric, approximately 1cm (½in) from the raw edge.

2 Take the needle through the interlining, at a diagonal from where you have just come out, thus forming the first side of the pyramid. You come out again 1cm (½in) from where you went into the interlining.

3 Now stitch back onto the main fabric, again approximately 1cm (½in) from the raw edge.

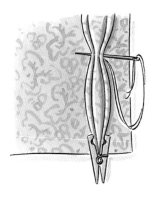

Stab Stitch

1 Using matching doubled thread, pass the needle backwards and forwards through your pleat. Push the needle straight through all the layers of fabric and repeat four times to make a strong and secure closure. You are below the fusible buckram here. With each stitch you make, you step nearer the fold of the pleats.

Suppliers

UK

Lady Caroline Wrey
66 Mysore Road
London SW11 5SB
Telephone: 0171-622 6625
Fax: 0171-787 0419
(*Fabric clamps, folding rulers, small metal rulers, long pins and long needles*)

Ciment Pleating
39b Church Hill Road
Church Hill
London E17 9RX
Telephone: 0181-520 0415
(*Permanent pleating*)

Elite (Mr Bushky)
27 Churton Street
London SW11 5SB
Telephone: 0171-622 6625
Fax: 0171-787 0419
(*Cleaning*)

Hallis Hudson Group Ltd
Bushell Street
Preston
Lancashire PR1 2SP
Telephone: 01772-202202
Fax: 01772-889889
(*Plain coloured chintzes*)

Hesse & Co
7 Warple Mews
Warple Way
London W3 0RF
Telephone: 0181-746 1366
Fax: 0181-746 2366
(*Interlinings and linings*)

Holbein
Wrafton Works
Rear of 45 Evelyn Road
London SW19 8NT
Telephone: 0181-542 2422
Fax: 0181-542 5222
(*Highly decorative curtain poles*)

Hunter & Hyland Ltd
201-205 Kingston Road
Leatherhead
Surrey KT2 7PB
Telephone: 01372-378511
Fax: 01372-370038
(*Interlinings, linings and curtain hanging materials*)

John Lewis Partnership
(*all branches*)
278 Oxford Street
London W1A 1EX
Telephone: 0171-629 7711
Fax: 0171-629 0849
(*Sewing equipment, fabrics, sheeting, haberdashery and curtain hanging materials*)

Johanna Long
36 Ash Road
Three Bridges
Crawley
West Sussex RH10 1SH
Telephone: 01293-524647
(*Tassels to order*)

Anne Ogden
Barnsnape House
Warninglid
West Sussex RH17 5SL
Telephone: 01444-461599
(*Headboards and trellised noticeboards to order*)

Alan Parker
23 Kelso Place
London W8 5QG
Telephone: 0171-937 6056
(*Screens to order*)

Pam Peterson
Balldown Farmhouse
Northwood Park
Starsholt
Hampshire S021 2LZ
Telephone: 01962-776368
(*Silk lampshades to order*)

Porter Nicholson
Portland House
Norlington Road
Leyton E10 6JX
Telephone: 0181-539 6106
Fax: 0181-558 9200
(*Interlinings and linings*)

Ramm, Son & Crocker
28 Chelsea Harbour
   Design Centre
Chelsea Harbour
Lotts Road
London SW10 0XE
Telephone: 0171-352 0931
Fax: 0171-352 0935
(*Furnishing fabrics, including most of those shown in this book*)

GJ Turner and Co
Fitzroy House
Abbot Street
London E8 3DP
Telephone: 0171-254 8187
Fax: 0171-245 8471
(*Trimmings*)

Brian Wright Esq
PO Box 2
24 Vernon Road
Falmouth
Cornwall TR11 3XB
Telephone: 01326-314448
(*Covered buttons*)

USA

ArtMark Fabric
480 Lancaster Pike
Frazer
PA 19355
Telephone: 1-800-523 0362
(*Plain coloured chintzes*)

Beacon Hill Showrooms
D&D Building
979 3rd Avenue
New York
NY 10022
Telephone: 212-421 1200
Fax: 212-826 5053
(*Furnishing fabrics, including most of those shown in this book*)

Calico Corners
(*national chain*)
745 Lancaster Pike
Strafford
Wayne
PA 19087
Telephone: 215-688 1505
(*Fabrics and sewing equipment*)

Cleantex Process Co Inc
2335 12th Avenue
New York
NY 10027
Telephone: 212-283 1200
(*Cleaners*)

DownRight Ltd
6101 16th Avenue
Brooklyn
NY 11204
Telephone: 718-232 2206
(*Cleaners*)

Gige Interiors Ltd
170 South Main Street
Yardley
PA 19067
Telephone: 215-493 8052
(*Interlinings, linings, plain coloured chintzes and curtain hanging materials*)

Graber Products Division
Springs Window Fashions
Middleton
WI 53562
Telephone: 1-800-322 9555
(*Curtain hanging materials*)

Greentext Upholstery Supplies
236 West 26th Street
New York
NY 1001
Telephone: 212-206 8585
(*Fabric clamps and folding rulers*)

Kirsch Co
PO Box 370
Sturges
MI 49091
Telephone: 1-800-528 1407
(*Curtain hanging materials*)

M&J Trimmings
1008 6th Avenue
New York
NY 10018
Telephone: 212-391 9072
(*Trimmings*)

George Matuk
37 West 26th Street
New York
NY 10010
Telephone: 212-683 9242
(*Sheeting*)

Norbar Fabrics
7670 Northwest 6th Avenue
Boca Raton
Florida 33487
Telephone: 1-800-645 8501
(*Plain coloured chintzes*)

SF Pleating
5th Floor
425 2nd Street
San Francisco
CA 94107
Telephone: 415-982 3003
(*Permanent pleating*)

Author's Acknowledgements

I want to thank my husband for his continued loving support and enthusiasm over the production of another book. Writing this book with Kate Haxell, my editor, has been nothing but fun and amusement. Her talent, enthusiasm and motivation gives me enormous strength and energy. I want to thank Cindy Richards and Kate Kirby for believing in me so positively and faithfully, and Cameron Brown and Mark Collins for continuing to want to publish me.

I would not have been able to write this book without the conscientious spirit, the invaluble knowledge and huge skills of Anne Ogden, Pam Peterson, Johanna Long and Alan Parker. I am extremely grateful to Marion Petschi and Amanda Hales who have helped so much in the production of many of the projects.

I also want to thank Lucinda Symons and Lucinda Egerton for their brilliantly skilled artistry in their photography and styling respectively. They have both been a real pleasure to work with and both have a way of filling one with huge confidence that whatever picture they are taking will be deeply successful. My thanks also to Janet James, our book designer, for making each page look so wonderful.

I want to thank Ramm, Son & Crocker for their great generosity with their wonderful fabric collections and Sarah Bennet for the dedication of so much of her time and effort to helping us with our choices of fabrics. All the fabrics shown on the *Fabric Chic* pages (unless otherwise stated) are Ramm, Son & Crocker fabrics, and these pages include the fabrics used for the projects in this book.
I want to thank Sam Lloyd for making all the step-by-step photography so much fun and Sonia Pugh for her enormous energy in promoting this book. I am very grateful to John Valencia (The Dormy House) who has continued to be so generous with his products for this book – namely the MDF screen for the *Gothic Screen* project. I want to thank Gayle Warwick of Warwick Fine Linen for so generously lending such utterly beautiful linen for the photoshoots.

Lady Caroline Wrey and Collins & Brown would also like to thank the following companies for lending items for the photography for this book.

Brora
344 King's Road
London SW3 5UR
Telephone: 0171-352 3697
(*Woollen blanket*)

The Bradley Collection
Lion Barn
Maitland Road
Needham Market
Suffolk IP6 8NS
Telephone: 01449-722726
(*Curtain pole*)

Cologne & Cotton
74 Regent Street
Leamington Spa
Warwickshire CV32 4NS
Telephone: 01926-332573
(*Bottles of cologne*)

Lavande Antiques
53 High Street, Battle
East Sussex TN33 0EN
Telephone: 01424-774474
(*Chairs, basket and wirework urn*)

The General Trading Company
144 Sloane Square
London SW1X 9BC
Telephone: 0171-730 0411
(*Boxes, lamps and glassware*)

Warwick Fine Linen
58 Eccleston Square
London SW1V 1PH
Telephone: 0171-592 9044
(*Embroidered bedlinen*)

Woodwrights
128-130 Lordship Lane
East Dulwich
London SE22 8HD
Telephone: 0181-299 4164
(*Candlestick, throw and rug*)

Index